**Kurt Vonnegut opens the Shain Library
(the "Noodle Factory," as he dubbed it in his remarks)**

photo credit Vincent Scarano.

This festschrift was first presented at "Centennial Celebration of William Meredith: His Legacy of Writing at Connecticut College" April 12, 2019 by the William Meredith Foundation and Poets' Choice Publishing. (WilliamMeredithFoundation.org and Poets-Choice.com)

William as a young professor at Connecticut College in the 1950's

EDITOR'S NOTE

FESTSCHRIFT FOR WILLIAM was produced to thank Connecticut College for remembering William Meredith this way, and for old friends there who have not forgotten his contribution to the college and our culture.

Poets' Choice wishes to thank *Poet Lore* for permission to use Collier's essay in this publication as well as my "Tribute" Volume 113 Number 3/4. Collier's work appears in Volume 114 1/2.

Love Song for William Meredith, Copyright © 2019 by Julia Alvarez. First published in CC: Connecticut College Magazine, Vol. 27 No. 3, Summer 2019. By permission of Stuart Bernstein Representation for Artists, New York, NY and protected by the Copyright Laws of the United States. All rights reserved. The printing, copying, redistribution, or retransmission of this Content without express permission is prohibited.

We also gratefully appreciate the contribution by Janet Gezari, J. Scott Price, Tom Kirlin and Krassin Himmirski for their insights into William Meredith and his work.

Richard Harteis

Poets-choice.com
WilliamMeredithFoundation.org

Copyright © 2019, Richard Harteis

ISBN-13: 978-1-7335400-2-5

CONTENTS

Acknowledgments and editorial comment	P. 3
Memorial Moment by Janet Gezari	P. 6
Just a Few Influences on William Meredith, J. Scott Price	P. 10
The Language of the Tribe by Michael Collier	P. 43.
ENABLING LOVE, Tom Kirlin	P. 53
MEREDITH POEMS	P. 157
ETCHINGS BY STOIMEN STOILOV	P. 170
Hundredth Anniversary by Krassin Himmirski	P. 171
A Tribute, by Richard Harteis	P. 178
A Love Song for William Meredith, Julia Alvarez	P. 182
Photo Gallery	P. 189

Sketch of William by Jeanne Meinke

Memorial Minute: William Meredith

by Janet Gezari

William Morris Meredith was born in New York City on January 9, 1919 and died on May 30, 2007 at Lawrence & Memorial Hospital after an illness of some weeks. He received a Pulitzer Prize in 1988 for Partial Accounts: New and Selected Poems, a National Book Award in 1997 for Effort at Speech: New and Selected Poems,
and many other awards, including fellowships and grants from the National Endowment for the Arts and the Guggenheim, Ford, and Rockefeller Foundations. He was a chancellor of the Academy of American Poets and served as Consultant in Poetry to the Library of Congress, a position re-titled Poet Laureate in 1985. He published nine volumes of poetry as well as Shelley: Selected Poems, Poets of Bulgaria, and Alcools, poems by Guillaume Apollinaire that he translated.

William earned his BA at Princeton University in 1940, where he followed his father and grandfather. He wrote his senior thesis on Robert Frost, who was a lasting influence on his poems and, later, a friend. Our library has a copy of the senior thesis, An Analysis of the Poetic Method of Robert Frost, inscribed by Frost, with gratitude, in 1940. The inscription suggests that Frost hadn't read the thesis and also says why: "I am assured on the best authority his results are very good. No man is supposed to look at himself in the glass except to shave." This was a view with which William would have concurred: "Study something deeper than yourselves" is how he puts it in one of his own poems.

After Princeton, William worked briefly for The New York Times (some of the obituaries said as a reporter, but I always understood he was a copy boy) before enlisting in the U. S. Army, and then the Navy, where he served as a pilot, making night landings on the decks of carriers. He re-enlisted for the Korean War, achieved the rank of Lieutenant Commander, and was awarded two Air Medals.
His formally precocious first book of poems, Love Letter from an Impossible Land was selected by Archibald MacLeish for the Yale Series of Younger Poets and published in 1944. Between active service in the Pacific and Korea, he did graduate work and taught English as a Woodrow Wilson fellow at Princeton and at the University of Hawaii. At Princeton, he met and became close friends with Charles Shain, who was also doing graduate work in English there. Much later, when Rosemary Park was due to retire here, William lured Charlie to Connecticut College, where he served as President from 1962 to 1974.

William began teaching at Connecticut College in 1955. In the mid 1960s, when Upward Bound programs were a fresh idea, he founded and taught in the college's first enrichment program for low-income inner city high school students. He taught until his retirement in 1983, after a stroke that immobilized him for two years and left him with lasting expressive aphasia. It was difficult for those of us who knew him well to fix the boundaries between what he understood and what he could say, although it often appeared that his apprehension of the world remained full and satisfying, and that only his capacity to articulate it was affected. I can remember afternoons in Uncasville, in the early years after the stroke, when I and several of my colleagues took turns reading poetry to William and helping him with the exercises in the speech manuals provided for his rehabilitation. If I missed a word in a poem or put the stress in the wrong place, he would stop me; meanwhile, the manuals had him reciting simple commands using the smallest number of linguistic units. The irony of his situation did not escape his notice, but it never diminished his resolve. Those who knew him after the stroke will remember his courage in the face of obstacles and his optimism about his progress. During this time and until his death, William was loved and cared for by his partner, the poet and fiction writer Richard Harteis.

Only those who knew William before the stroke know the magnitude of his loss, and ours. William was consummately articulate, and his conversation was one of the highest pleasures of his company. His letters, typed on his old manual machine if he was at home or handwritten if he was traveling, spoke about cadged meals, boozy evenings with friends, and the cornus alternifolia (or alternate-leafed dogwood) he thought you ought to have in your garden. He told wonderful stories and liked elaborate jokes. He was effortlessly and often savagely witty. His judgment of language was impeccable and accounts in part for his centrality to what was then the world of American poetry. William knew all the poets, and several of his more celebrated contemporaries—Robert Penn Warren, John Berryman, and Robert Lowell—relied on his responses to their poems and drafts of poems. While he was here, William saw to it that poetry was a part of life at Connecticut College. In addition to the writers I've just mentioned, Derek Walcott, Thom Gunn, Muriel Rukeyser, Eudora Welty, Maxine Kumin, Richard Wilbur, and Robert Frost all came to New London to give readings. Afterwards, there were long dinners in Uncasville where conversation flowed as generously as the drinks did. William was most his own strange self when he was hosting one of these dinners. He believed that food was meant to be served, and served with love. He wasn't particular about what we ate but he was very particular about how we did it. Stacking the dishes when you helped to clear the table was never permitted. During the thirteen years I was William's colleague, I don't remember his taking a sabbatical, but when he did take time away to teach at Carnegie Mellon or to perform his duties at the Library of Congress, he would produce his substitute. I remember all of these replacements well because they made extraordinary contributions to the life of the English department and the college. Blanche Boyd was one; the others were a former student and widely published writer of historical fiction, Cecilia Holland; the distinguished poet Robert Hayden, who had been the first black poet to serve as Poetry Consultant at the Library of Congress; the playwright Romulus Linney; and the Pulitzer Prize winning short story writer, James Alan MacPherson.

It was a mark of William's humility that his own poetry readings always combined a few of his poems with a larger number of poems written by other poets. He had no truck with grade inflation, and he used a teacher's shorthand when he described himself as a B+ poet who had written a few A plus poems. In the eulogy he gave at William's funeral, Michael Collier, William's former student and now a poet and teacher of poetry at the University of Maryland, reminded us that William used to say that he was proud of only three things: his knowledge of prosody, his knowledge of trees, and his immunity to poison ivy. His knowledge of prosody and trees was immense, as was his knowledge of many other things human and natural. He knew, for example, a lot about music, and had been opera critic for the Hudson Review, but he wore his knowledge lightly. He was always more interested in what you could tell him than in what he could tell you.

No one could have fought harder against death than William did, and this was entirely consistent with the life he had led and the poems he had written. He felt himself bound to continue, whether he was flying a mission for the Navy or composing a sestina. He feared cowardice more than other terrors, but he also felt grateful for the beauty of the universe and never stopped being conscious of its particular kindness to him. A poem titled "John and Anne" takes John Berryman's words about Anne Frank as its epigraph: "the hardest challenge, let's say, that a person can face without defeat is the best for him." Just outside the door to William's house in Uncasville, there was a tamarack tree that had been savagely cropped by an oil truck. He liked to point out that the accident had made the tree thrive as it never could have otherwise.

William Meredith was the least suicidal poet of his generation. His last book of new poems, published a few years before his stroke, was titled The Cheer, an improbable title for any poet but William. The first poem in the book, a kind of envoi, goes like this:

Frankly, I'd like to make you smile Words addressing
evil won't turn evil back but they can give us heart.
The cheer is hidden in right words.

By cheer William means morale or confidence or, better still, courage, with its etymological connections to heart. He wanted us to be heartened, even though—or perhaps because—we live in "a culture in late imperial decline." The Cheer,
written during the Vietnam war, includes a poem in which the poet presents himself as a "mild-spoken citizen" and respectfully accuses his country's president of "criminal folly." "A man's mistakes," the poem slyly notes, "his worst acts,/ aren't out of character, as he'd like to think." The Cheer includes several elegies, wry and celebratory poems written in memory of Lowell, Hemingway, Plath, and Berryman. All of them except Lowell, who tried to kill himself more than once, succeeded in ending their own lives. William dreamed and imagined death over and over. The elegy had been an important kind of poem for him since "The Wreck of the Thresher," which he wrote to commemorate "a squad of brave men" who died at sea in 1963. If his career as a wartime pilot, someone who faced death down daily, provides one important context for his struggle to survive after his stroke, the too short lives of the poets he loved, past and present, provide the other.

In "Talking Back (To W. H. Auden)," William rejects Auden's idea (in his elegy for W. B. Yeats) that "poetry makes nothing happen." "What it makes happen is small things," his poem says. William's highest aspiration as a poet was always spiritual, but he was never solemn. He agreed with Frost that "all the fun's in how you say a thing." His most memorable poems enable us to see the most forgettable things newly and to be changed by what we've seen. In one of Tom Stoppard's plays, there's a sentence honoring the effort at speech that defined William's life: "If you get the right [words] in the right order, you can nudge the world a little or make a poem which children will speak for you when you die.

Just a Few of the Influences on William Meredith and His Poetry

By J. Scott Price

Advisor: Richard Jackson

Summer 2018

Submitted in partial fulfillment of the requirements of the Fine Arts in Writing Program at

Vermont College of Fine Arts

If one were to imagine a tragedy of Greek proportions that could befall a poet, losing the ability to speak and write would come in at the top of most of our lists. That tragedy could be further compounded by imagining it happening to a nationally recognized poet at the peak of his career. Yet that is exactly what happened to William Meredith in 1983, at the age of 64, when he suffered a stroke that left him unable to speak or move. Meredith, and his long-time partner Richard Harteis, were, of course, initially devastated by this life-altering physical loss, but the *joie de vivre* spirit and aplomb which sustained Mr. Meredith his entire life would not dissipate.

Friend to W.H Auden and Robert Frost, confidant of Robert Lowell and John Berryman, recognized as a blooming talent in poetry early in his life by Muriel Rukeyser and Allen Tate, held in high esteem (even to this day) in a country once snugly behind the Iron Curtain (Bulgaria), advocate for Robert Hayden, and a highly regarded professor for over 30 years who taught thousands of students over the course of his life, William Meredith was a poet of high intelligence and skill, with intimate knowledge of the poets who came before him that planted the seeds that would blossom to become Meredith's own style of articulate, intelligent verse.

He served as a Navy pilot in both WW2 and the Korean War, but rather than derail him from his poetic path, both of those wars were catalysts for his writing and career. His first book, *Love Letter from an Impossible Land*, was published during WW2, and he stated that his experience in the latter war reignited his stagnating writing career. He published nine poetry collections in his lifetime, won three awards from *Poetry* magazine, earned prestigious fellowships and grants (from Princeton, the Rockefeller Foundation, the NEA, the Ford Foundation, and a Guggenheim Fellowship), became the Consultant for Poetry at the Library of Congress from 1978-1980 (the position was later renamed U.S. Poet

Laureate in 1985), and taught at several distinguished universities. All of the above, with the exception of publishing his last two volumes, were done before he was felled by the stroke in 1983. But even that life-altering event did not derail his love of life or poetry.

Meredith and Harteis were not deterred—heartbroken, frustrated, and occasionally sad, yes—but not deterred, and they both worked daily on intense physical and speech therapy regimens (even travelling to Great Britain for specialized care) to regain as much of his previous physical ability as possible over the subsequent years. This diligence and indomitable spirit saw Meredith earn some of the literary world's most prestigious awards in the years that followed—five years after his stroke (1988) he earned the *L.A Times* Book Prize and Pulitzer Prize for *Partial Accounts: New and Selected Poems*. Nearly a decade later (1997), the same year that Charles Frazier's *Cold Mountain* won in Fiction and Frank Bidart's *Desire* was a finalist in poetry, William Meredith earned the National Book Award in Poetry for his *Effort at Speech*.[1]

I had not heard of William Meredith prior to beginning this semester (which just goes to show how the world of poetry can be a vast and ever-replenishing ocean that always has more to offer each new seeker). Even though I had developed what I thought were separate interests in what influences poets, and in poets with military experience, Meredith slipped past my radar until my faculty advisor suggested I look into him. As I conducted my initial research I discovered his story was the perfect confluence of what had already piqued my interests—a person who served in uniform and went on to become a distinguished poet, and one whose overt and covert influences on his life and literary career could be discerned with further research.

---

[1] http://www.nationalbook.org/nba1997.html#.W0paFdJKjIU, retrieved 20 August 2018.

In the introduction to Meredith's 1964 translation of French poet Guillaume Apollinaire's *Alcools* : *Poems 1898-1913,* Francis Steegmuller, American biographer of many French authors, states, "As in the case of all great poets, Apollinaire's life and poetry illuminate each other," [2] and this paper takes the same approach: illustrating how the life of William Meredith and his poetry were fully intertwined. His style, subject matter, and career-wide themes only unfolded as they did because of the life he lived.

It is difficult to capture and quantify the influences, direct and indirect, that determine the outcome of an individual life, and only slightly less difficult to try to do so for a famous poet. Each of us is unique, and each poet's voice similarly unique, but it is rare a poet's voice becomes entirely unique, because it is by default a product of not only that poet's unique life experiences, but also of all the literary influence that the poet consciously or unconsciously received as the poet strove to create better and better poems. However, we can begin to isolate some of the contributing factors that make a particular poet's voice unique enough to stand out from others.

The collection of Meredith' book reviews, essays, and presentations, *Poems Are Hard to Read,* is not widely circulated and was difficult to locate, and there have been very few essays or articles written about him and his works (compared to other major poets of his time and caliber). What few were written were done during his lifetime, with almost nothing written about him over the past 11 years since his death in 2007.

These factors may be indicators of his currently "lost" place in the world of poetry, but it has become clear in my research that he deserves a more prominent place at today's ever-expanding poetry table. He was respected and well regarded during his life, and his

---

[2] Apollinaire, Guillaume, and Francis Steegmuller. *Alcools : Poems, 1898-1913*. Translated by William Meredith, First ed., Doubleday & Company, 1964.p. v.

passing shouldn't diminish his status. But I also realize that poets ebb and flow in and out of favor over time, and perhaps his life after death has yet to begin—and very well may not ever. The odds are not stacked in any one writer's favor in this regard.

However, I propose to make a brief case for him, and to illustrate the how and why he became a poet, Naval aviator in two wars, a professor, and respected member the literary community, here and abroad. This is a short list, at the start of this paper, to attempt to capture the many competing and confluent influences on who Meredith was as a poet and a man. This paper is far too short to illustrate how each of these factors contributed to how his career developed as it did, but I will attempt to address a few of the more heavily weighted factors:

Environment

Upper class New England upbringing
Classical education (preparatory school and Princeton)
Aleutians Islands during WW2
River Thames, Uncasville, CT (home)
Religious upbringing and renewed interest later in life
Military training and experience
Bulgaria
High Intelligence

Passions
Trees
Birds
Opera

Poets & Allies

Muriel Rukeyser
Allen Tate
Robert Frost
Archibald MacLeish
W.H. Auden
Percy Blythe Shelley
W.B. Yeats
Emily Dickinson
John Berryman
Robert Lowell
Richard Harteis
Thomas Hardy
Guillaume Apollinaire

Meredith grew up in Darien, Connecticut "on the edge of Long Island Sound [and] spent summers in small boats."[3] His father was a well-to-do banker, not massively successful but fairly well off, and when Meredith was coming of age during the Depression, his family fared far better than most.

---

[3] Gerald, Gregory Fitz, et al. "The Frost Tradition: A Conversation with William Meredith." *Southwest Review*, vol. 57, no. 2, 1972, p. 109.

He attended the elite Lenox School for Boys in Lenox, Massachusetts (loosely affiliated with the Episcopal Church) for his four high school years, and was an A & B student in English and Science, and a C & D student in Latin, History, and Math, but he pulled up his final Senior year grades to all As and Bs.

As part of his Princeton application his headmaster rated him as "definitely better than average, perhaps low honor rating" with English studies being where he "probably" "exhibited special mental qualifications or unusual ability." He was the editor in chief of his school newspaper, was on the Newspaper Board, and the football team, as well as being a member of the Religious Society and manager of the baseball team.[4] The headmaster went on to note, though, "Bill has never been interested in athletics, or done well at them. It is much to his credit that he played on the football squad, and showed good spirit, though his accomplishments, so far as football was concerned was not very great." From an early age, Meredith's preferred playing field, like many fledgling poets, was the internal landscape of the mind.

His Princeton application's "General Estimate" essay, completed by his school's headmaster, shows "His I.Q. rating has been steadily in the 130-135 range," with steadily improving grades rising to meet that potential. "In the early years, he was a rather precocious youngster, given far too much to introspection and the desire to react in a grown up fashion to adults. His interests and inclinations were in no sense those typical of boyhood, nor are they now. He managed to cultivate a rather superior manner which generally gave considerable offence, and for teachers he had a most annoying placidity which it was almost impossible to ruffle." This last point undoubtedly helped him become

---

[4] Seeley G. Mudd Manuscript Library, Princeton, Box 44, Folder (William Meredith), Finding Aid AC198.03_c128

a successful naval aviator and can help explain his undaunted spirit after his life-altering stroke.

"He is much less of a 'lone wolf' than he was, though he is still not entirely comprehended by his form mates." This final assessment from his principal would always be true to some extent, but ever-lessening as he grew as a poet and a man, because Meredith recognized these—his introversion, high intelligence and education, and his "separateness" from peers—were issues for him to address early on, and he took measures to become more accessible and intimate with others throughout his life. Joining the military was his first step after Princeton, and becoming a trusted confidant and sounding board to fellow poets and students the rest of his life was part of his self-improvement "path that never ends."

By the end of his life, he had developed what was described as a "gift for friendship. And he radiated what I can describe only as an aura of humanity."[5] Michael Collier, a once-student and long-time friend of Meredith who went on to become a successful poet and professor, said during his eulogy that what made Meredith so impactful was "a deep interest in people and a belief that each of us wrestled with one or two or several demons; that we all possess flaws but were redeemed and ennobled by our efforts to face them."[6] My outsider's brief incursion into Meredith's life confirms these assessments.

Meredith wrote in his Princeton application, "The English course at Princeton, I

---

[5] Harte, Jack. *An Irishman's Diary: Jack Harte on William Meredith's pilgrimage to Yeats's Sligo.* Jan 6, 2015. https://www.irishtimes.com/culture/heritage/an-irishman-s-diary-jack-harte-on-william-meredith-s-pilgrimage-to-yeats-s-sligo-1.2055604, retrieved 28 July 2018

[6] Collier, Michael. "Eulogy for William Meredith." https://www.conncoll.edu/in-memoriam/william-meredith/eulogy-by-michael-collier/, retrieved 18 July 2018

feel, will be the most interesting, and useful one to me if my present interests are to be taken as a criterion, but the width of scope of the courses in the freshman and sophomore years may well change or supplement this present standard." He also notes, "I expect to meet people at Princeton whom I shall see later on in life if I live, as I expect to, in or around New York." He also references "a certain amount of tradition", as he was a Princeton legacy student, his grandfather graduating in 1877 and father graduating in 1911.[7]

Meredith was right. At Princeton he met and befriended the Dean, Christian Gauss, a friend of Meredith's father, who would play an ongoing mentor role in his life after Princeton; Charlie Shain '36, who Meredith helped bring to Connecticut College where he taught most of his career as its new President in 1962, and poet Allen Tate who would play a prominent role in his initial foray into the wider literary world.

It seems Meredith was interested in studying Military Science (what we now call the Reserve Officer Training Corp, ROTC) while at Princeton, but his father and preparatory school head master dissuaded him from this course of study before arriving a Princeton. However, just to be sure, Meredith's father wrote a familiar letter to the Princeton Director of Admissions, Radcliffe Heermance, in the fall of his freshman year. Meredith's father did not feel that this sort of training "has a place in a broad cultural training such as I want Bill to have at Princeton."[8] His father served in the American Expeditionary Force during the First World War [9], and it's entirely probable Meredith's father wanted to spare him from similar experiences, so there were to be no military studies

---

[7] Seeley G. Mudd Manuscript Library, Princeton, Box 44, Folder (William Meredith), Finding Aid AC198.03_c128
[8] Seeley G. Mudd Manuscript Library, Princeton, Box 44, Folder (William Meredith), Finding Aid AC198.03_c128
[9] Charles Shain Library archives, Connecticut College, Box 15, 29 Oct 18

at Princeton for William, and his suppressed military aspirations had to wait until after graduation in 1940—when the country was once again fully on a trajectory for war.

In his 60s, Meredith admitted be began writing poetry as early as eight years old, but student records indicate he went to Princeton for undergraduate work unclear what he wanted to do after earning his degree (or perhaps unwilling to admit to it). Even upon graduating with honors with an English degree in 1940 he was still unsure, and stated in his yearbook that he would "probably engage in the publishing business." He had already been contributing to and helping edit the school's literary journal, *Nassau Lit,* as well as contributing to *the Daily Princetonian* as a columnist. He ran cross country and tutored History 101-2 for two years. He was writing poetry consistently at this time, and was honored with being asked to write his graduating class poem, which he subsequently published in his first book.

The Creative Arts Program at Princeton was founded during Meredith's final year at Princeton under the direction of his friend and mentor Dean Christian Gauss, who took the young Meredith under his wing (as much as time and circumstances allowed) while at Princeton, taught at least one class to Meredith, and who remained a correspondent and supporter of Meredith until Gauss's death in 1951. The Creative Arts Program was originally funded by a five-year grant from the Carnegie Corporation before transitioning into a permanent Princeton department. It was this program that brought in the then famous poet and critic Allen Tate that same year to work with talented writing students,[10] and it was Tate who saw great promise in Meredith and who provided the conduit (and most likely significant encouragement) for Meredith's first manuscript to find its way to

---

[10] http://etcweb.princeton.edu/CampusWWW/Companion/creative_arts_program.html, retrieved 7-28-18

Archibald MacLeish, who ultimately chose *Love Letters from an Impossible Land* as the winner of the Yale Series of Younger Poets Prize for 1944.

Princeton is highly selective today, and was just as selective, if not more so, during Meredith's undergraduate time there (1936-1940). Following the First World War there was a boom in college applications across institutions in America, and in 1922 Princeton adopted "a policy of limited enrollment and selective admission in order to preserve the essential features of Princeton's residential life and to maintain its standards of individual instruction."[11] While there were a few outliers prior, Princeton did to begin recruiting racial minorities and women until the mid-to-late 1960s, so most of Meredith's peers and professors came from the same higher-end socio-economic and geographic background as himself. This blue-blood pedigree, just like his "lone wolf" instinct, were two aspects of his personality (and which conveyed into his early writing) that he intentionally tried to diminish over time (he was once "placed among the caustic aristocrats of American verse").[12] He understood himself, and who he wanted to be, and took active measures as his career progressed to grow as a poet and a man. "And I've realized that there's a certain way you can be snobbishly grown up; Frost's poems never had that quality, but mine used to."[13]

America was attacked by the Japanese on December 7, 1941 but America's eventual involvement in the growing worldwide conflagration had been apparent to many

---

[11] http://etcweb.princeton.edu/CampusWWW/Companion/admissions.html, retrieved 7-28-18

[12] Young, Vernon, et al. "Poetry Chronicle: The Light is Dark enough." *The Hudson Review* 34.1 (1981): 141. Print. p.149

[13] Gerald, Gregory Fitz, et al. "The Frost Tradition: A Conversation with William Meredith." *Southwest Review*, vol. 57, no. 2, 1972, p. 115.

since the Nazis invaded Poland in 1939. Meredith's previous inclinations towards military studies and his knowledge of world history and affairs made it apparent that he, and most others of his generation, would eventually serve in uniform. However, familial reticence is hard to overcome, so upon graduation he took a "copy boy" position at the *New York Times*. About a year later, in May 1941, before we'd officially entered the war, Meredith enlisted in the Army as a private and rose quickly the few steps to corporal, eventually working in public relations after his initial entry training until January of 1942. In a November 13, 1941 letter to Meredith, Dean Gauss wrote, "I wish I could tell you how much it means to me to us here to see recent Alumni of your character and capacity so willing and eager to do their part." This sort of positive reinforcement from a man Meredith so admired must have buoyed him in his long-held desire to serve in uniform despite the previously noted disapproval of his father.

Meredith's writing skills helped him rise quickly in Army public relations, but that wasn't where he wanted to be. Meredith wanted wings. In June of 1942 Dean Gauss of Princeton was asked for a character reference as part of Meredith's background investigation for transferring to Navy aviation. The Dean wrote in reply that Meredith did "unusually able work" while his student, and that "Few men showed deeper and more wholehearted devotion to their country than he," and that Meredith was "less interested in a commission than in doing his duty." This is exactly the type of endorsement one would expect, but it still speaks highly of young Meredith.

In his 40's and 60's Meredith wrote a few poems about his mother, but rarely about his father. Other than the issue of military service, and the to-be-expected father/son conflicts that occur as a younger man grows into his own individuality, there might have been other issues where the young Meredith did not receive his father's approval, and we can look to the Oct/Nov 1962 *Poetry* for insight into what their interactions might very well have been like over time.

For His Father

When I was young I looked high and low for a father,
And what blond sons you must have tried on then!
But only your blood could give us our two men
And in the end we settled for one another.

Whatever death is, it sets pretenders free.
The secret loss or boyhood or self-defense
That won me your affectionate pretense
Is in a grave. Now you judge only me.

But like a living son I go on railing
A little, or praising under my breath,
Not knowing the generosity of death,
Fearing your judgement on my old failing.

Dear ghost, take pleasure in our good report,
And bully me no further with my blame.
You use my eyes at last; I sign your name
Deliberately beneath my life and art.

The emotional complexity and precise word use override the poem's form, and the subtle rhymes of the A B B A quatrain seem almost undetected during the initial reading. Shame, pride, rebellion, grief, acceptance, judgement, and undeterrable-despite-it-all love all equally come through in these few, short, highly crafted and emotionally charged lines. The reader need not have any prior knowledge to detect the complications of this father-son relationship.

Just nine months after entering the military, in February 1942, he was accepted into the Navy for aviator training, and served on active duty until February 1946, demobilizing about six months after the war ended in the Pacific. Perhaps it was growing up on the water near boats that prodded him to leave the Army for Naval aviation, but it was more likely the chance to use his intellect to greater purpose and the challenge that entailed. In 2003, James Bradly published *Flyboys : A True Story of Courage*, chronicling the experiences of Naval Aviators in the Pacific: "These airmen would go to war sitting down. As warriors they were prized not for their brawn but for their brains. Throngs of fighting men were trained not to develop calluses but to master syllabi. Navigation, dead reckoning, map reading, code recognition, and myriad mechanical challenges faced these Flyboys." [14] Meredith would make good use of his intelligence with these colleagues. Also, I believe, much of the "precocious" and "lone wolf" aspect of Meredith's personality remained intact this early into his military career, and relying on his own intelligence and instincts as a pilot likely had greater appeal than being an anonymous member of a larger team in the Army.

In an interesting case of what-might-have-been, Meredith had requested to remain in uniform on active duty following the end of WW2, but his request was denied, so he went on to teach poetry as a Woodrow Wilson Fellow at Princeton (where he was an assistant to the well-known poetry critic and professor R. P. Blackmur and began publishing book reviews of his own), and the University of Hawaii between the wars. His first book, *Love Letters from an Impossible Land*, came out during WW2 (compiled by two of his friends back home while he served in the Aleutians Islands off the Alaskan coast) and his second book, *Ships and Other Figures,* was published in 1948 during the fellowship at Princeton.

Order, poetic form, is the sense by which Meredith experiences all poetry. When discussing his own and other's works, he always goes back to how a poem embraces, disregards, or returns to order. In a 1983 interview with Ed Hirsch (published in 1985), he

---

[14] Bradley, James. *Flyboys : A True Story of Courage*. 1st ed., Little, Brown, 2003. p.123

said he saw himself as a "lyric poet" and only made poems "out of insights I encounter," and "I wait until the poems seem to be addressed not to 'Occupant' but to 'William Meredith'", and "I think…poetry and experience should have an exact ratio".[15] All of these are precise guidelines for how he writes, perceives, and relates to poetry. There is order and then there is chaos. Meredith's poetry was clearly in the order camp.

While this may be attributed to his upbringing and simply to his own poetry aesthetic, it is also highly likely contributed to by his military training. The military is designed to function in chaotic environments, and has often been referred to as "organized chaos." All branches use highly organized systems to facilitate operations, and pilots most significantly rely on systems and checklists to mitigate errors. When lives are on the line, attention to detail is paramount—order saves lives.

Order is also reflected in the traditional forms used by the poets he studied and were influenced by in his youth—Hardy, Yeats, Auden, Shelley. Many of his early poems were in traditional forms and he was fairly established in his career before began writing outside of these traditional forms. Former student and friend Collier said that "William's insistence on form was the verbal equivalence of manners, the enacting of ceremony, protocols really for controlling the emotions that lay beneath the experience at hand…Form was rooted in his life."[16]

Later in his life he credited Robert Frost for helping him venture from what he called "borrowed rhetoric" of his early work, but he always kept traditional forms close to

---

[15] Hirsch, Edward, and William Meredith. "The Art of Poetry XXXIV : William Meredith." *Paris review* (1985) Print. p.39

[16] Collier, Michael. "Eulogy for William Meredith." https://www.conncoll.edu/in-memoriam/william-meredith/eulogy-by-michael-collier/, retrieved 18 July 2018

his heart and style. As poet and professor Linda Gregerson noted in her 1988 review of his second to last book, *Partial Accounts* : "Here is a poet who asks us seriously to consider the rhymed quatrain as a unit of perceptual pacing, the villanelle as the ambivalent and ritual simulation of fate, the sestina as a scaffolding for directed ruminations, the sonnet as an instrument for testing the prodigious or the ineffable against the long-for-shapeliness we know as 'argument'." She goes on, "Meredith has a habit of talking back to his elders. He writes in alliterative tercets that hearken back to the very beginning of poetry in English" and "He pursues in rhymed trimeter an Audenesque intractability." [17]

What the reviewer did not note is that he also not only models previous poets in *Partial Accounts,* he directly references and interacts with them ("Talking Back (To W.H. Auden)" and "What I Remember the Writers Telling Me When I Was Young" (for Muriel Rukeyser)." Poets have a long history of writing a poem in response to a previous poem from another poet. We use poetry to argue or agree with voices of the past, and sometimes to pay them tribute. The effect of both of these poems is of overhearing the speaker talking to himself about these influential people in his life—the reader sensing the speaker imagining them again into life—and the speaker giving him their due in words that will outlive them all.

In a couple of his books he provided prose explanatory statements with his poems, to give the reader details to assist them understanding the poem, and he likens this to what a poet might say during a reading to set the stage and help the audience better understand

---

[17] Gregerson, Linda. "Book Review: Partial Accounts: New and Selected Poems." *Poetry* 151.5 (1988): 423-426. Print. (p.423-424)

what they're about to digest.[18] Most of these notes were related to military terminology and operations, but not exclusively—occasionally he would do this for literature he references in his poems. He received mixed reviews for this practice, and it mostly fell off in his latter books, but he couldn't curb this practice completely, and it was used a few times in his final book. Again, order prevails in Meredith's poetry.

The vocabulary he uses in his poems is evidence of his Princeton education and is another reinforcing factor for his reputation as an "academic" poet. He was known for his "exacting diction which has heretofore been a signature."[19] He can't escape his education and intelligence; it keeps bubbling up in his writing his entire life. Though he never truly tried to escape it, he did try to make it less apparent at certain points.

He always seemed to think of himself as a "B" poet, or "minor poet" (even referring to himself as such in *Efforts at Speech's* poem "Grace"), despite a plethora of awards and external validation on the quality of his verse. I believe this was in part due to the wide acclaim his good friends received during their lifetimes (Lowell, Berryman, Auden, Frost), but also in part due to the high acclaim those he was inspired by, and influenced by, received (Yeats, Frost, Shelley, Auden, Keats). But this consideration of himself as such wasn't from self-pity, but rather from what he believed to be an honest, intellectually unbiased assessment of his place on the rung of poetry (with also a strong dose of professional-fronting humility masking a strong sense of self-confidence, but the manners of a gentlemen as he conceived himself to be (and was), encouraged a certain

---

[18] Gerald, Gregory Fitz, et al. "The Frost Tradition: A Conversation with William Meredith." *Southwest Review*, vol. 57, no. 2, 1972, pp. 115.

[19] Young, Vernon, et al. "Poetry Chronicle: The Light is Dark enough." *The Hudson Review* 34.1 (1981): 141. Print. p.149

level of public modesty). He went on in the poem "Grace" to use humor effectively to take the sting out his self-assessment, writing: "Finally, you will have to look me up / in the joust of modern poets / where my pen name, *Lancelitle,* / may not yet have been appeared, / or already have been expunged…"

On the matter of grace, Meredith consistently demonstrated the gentlemanly decorum for which he was known in his poems, lectures, essays, criticism, and interviews. When asked by an interviewer to agree that Robert Frost was harsh under certain circumstances, he asked the interviewer, "Are you a harsh man under certain circumstances?" with the obvious answer from the interviewer being, "Yes." "Well," Meredith replied, "that far I'll go. He was also, as you know, secretly very generous to people." And when reflecting on less-than-glowing reviews authors sometimes receive, he did not espouse animosity towards critics, only right-sized self-reflection, "Reviews are helpful, I think, only in telling you what misunderstandings you have allowed range for." [20]

Previous literature plays a huge role in the subject and form of many of Meredith's poems. Meredith received a Guggenheim Fellowship in 1975/76 and used it in a detailed study of Percy Blythe Shelley, Edward Trelawny, Joseph Severn, and John Keats. [21] He had already co-edited a book in 1968 with Randall Jarrell's first wife, *Eighteenth-Century English Minor Poets,* and now wanted to dig deeper on his own into the lives of these few late 19th Century men. After the springboard of the Fellowship, he spent the latter half of the 70's "writing about Edward John Trelawny, the friend of Shelley and Byron" and published the poem "English Accounts" in 1997's *Effort at Speech* (a previous version was titled "Trelawny's Dream").

---

[20] Gerald, Gregory Fitz, et al. "The Frost Tradition: A Conversation with William Meredith." *Southwest Review*, vol. 57, no. 2, 1972, pp. 114-116
[21] Email correspondence with the Guggenheim Foundation, received 29 October 2018

Widespread criticism of Trelawny paints the picture of a liar, poser, and possible con-man, responsible for Shelley's death (reasonably undisputed), not the dashing world-travelling corsair and adventurer he wanted his literary benefactors, and the world, to believe himself to be. Meredith defends Trelawny, though. "He was an outsize and attractively outrageous man, and probably only the fact that I managed to survive, in character, a friendship with Frost emboldens me to keep Trelawny for an imaginary playmate." Meredith wanted to write "a series of poems" about him, in part because, "I have come to like and believe him. I believe he tells by and large generous truths about Shelley and Byron, the former of whom he idolized, the latter of whom he saw plain…a temporarily unfashionable position…"[22] So we see the intertwining of a modern literary figure (Frost) and ones from the past (Byron, Shelley, Trelawny) influencing his work and sense of self.

I propose that part of this fascination with Trelawny is that Meredith saw himself as the same sort of hanger-on to great men of his time, rather than as one himself. As mentioned earlier, to himself and those closest to him he referred to himself as a B poet, and most of his poems the same—better than most but always "just" short of the mark. From the same poem, "English Accounts", Meredith, in the guise of Trelawny, writes "Though I am still a strong swimmer / I can feel the channel widen as I swim." Meredith/Trelawny think they are progressing towards their goals, but the goals always remain ever just out of reach. We hear this sentiment repeated by successful people from all walks of life, especially of the creative variety, so I can see how Meredith would have felt slightly inadequate and seemingly never progressing—even though he was just around the corner from being named the Consultant for Poetry at the Library of Congress.

---

[22] Reasons for Poetry and The Reason for Criticism. Two Lectures Delivered at the Library of Congress on May 7, 1979 and May 5, 1980. Retreived 27 July 2018.

The influence of one poet on another can change over time, as the receiving poet changes and grows, and the preceding poet no longer speaks the same way to the emerging poet. Yeats is one such influence on Meredith, who read a lot of him during WW2 but not much after. Meredith's "The Chinese Banyan" (From 1958's *The Open Sea*) is in the same form, iambic trimeter, as Yeats' "The Fisherman."[23] It is easy to understand how Meredith might have felt compelled to move away from his earlier influences as he gained prominence and began pushing his own boundaries (the natural trajectory for a poet's growth, but it's hard to suppress the pull of a first love). Yeats' influence might have waned in Meredith's middle years, but Meredith did take a 2006 pilgrimage at the age of 87 to Yeats' home turf. He told his host that Yeats was his favorite poet and repeatedly stated, ""I am 87, and I am in Ireland. I am a happy man." Richard Harteis, Meredith's life partner, said it was the fulfillment of a life-long dream for Meredith.[24]

In speaking of his influences during an April 7, 1971 interview, Meredith states:

> The ocean and trees strike me as being parts of natural experience that make metaphors in the head when you're sleeping, or when you're at the edge of consciousness, where poems come from. And I've become more and more fastidious about wanting to know what's happening there. I know a little bit about the ocean, I know a good deal more about trees, not because I'm attempting to flee from technological society, but because that seems to me where it's at in the terms of my imagination.[25]

I believe the impact of the ocean in his writing is fairly well known and evident, given his first few books and their prominent Navy/Ocean/Sea subject matter and titles

---

[23] Gerald, Gregory Fitz, et al. "The Frost Tradition: A Conversation with William Meredith." *Southwest Review*, vol. 57, no. 2, 1972, p. 116.

[24] Harte, Jack. *An Irishman's Diary: Jack Harte on William Meredith's pilgrimage to Yeats's Sligo.* Jan 6, 2015. https://www.irishtimes.com/culture/heritage/an-irishman-s-diary-jack-harte-on-william-meredith-s-pilgrimage-to-yeats-s-sligo-1.2055604, retrieved 28 July 2018

[25] Gerald, Gregory Fitz, et al. "The Frost Tradition: A Conversation with William Meredith." *Southwest Review*, vol. 57, no. 2, 1972, p. 109.

(*The Open Sea, Ships and Other Figures, The Wreck of the Thresher*). What is less evident, given that the references are sprinkled throughout his works and rarely included in poem titles, is that over the course of his career, he mentions specific types of trees in a significantly large portion of his poems, and used trees allegorically in love poems. It wasn't until I walked the grounds of Connecticut College where he taught for so many years that I fully understood the Meredith-Tree relationship. The grounds are nothing but magnificent tree varieties, and the college is known for its 750-acre arboretum (began in 1931) and botany programs. Surely this played a role in his choice of teaching locations. He was a hobby arborist, and his home on the Thames river in CT was his personal lab.

Tree Marriage

In Chota Nagpur and Bengal
the betrothed are tied with threads to
mango trees, they marry the trees
as well as one another, and
the two trees marry each other.
Could we do that some time with oaks
or beeches? This gossamer we
hold each other with, this web
of love and habit is not enough.
In mistrust of heavier ties,
I would like tree-siblings for us,
standing together somewhere, two
trees married with us, lightly, their
fingers barely touching in sleep,
our threads invisible but holding.

A Couple of Trees

The two oaks lean apart for light.
They aren't as strong as lone oaks
but in a wind they give each other lee.

Daily since I cleared them I can see
them, tempting to chain saw and ax–
two hardwoods, leaning like that for light.

A hurricane tore through the state one night,

picking up roof and hen-house, boat and dock.
These two stood: leafless, twigless, giving lee.

Last summer ugly slugs unleafed the trees.
Environmental kids wrote *Gypsy Moths Suck*.
The V of naked oaks leaned to the light

for a few weeks, then put out slight
second leaves, scar tissue pale as bracts,
bandaged comrades, lending each other lee.

How perilous in one another's V
our lives are, yoked in this yoke:
two men, leaning apart for light,
but in a wind who give each other lee.

One need look no further than the opening lines of Frost's *Birches* (published in 1916), and one of Meredith's early idols, to see similarities—first person narration, nature's impact on the subject trees and the imaginative journey that begins with these observations:

When I see birches bend to left and right
Across the lines of straighter darker trees,
I like to think some boy's been swinging them.
But swinging doesn't bend them down to stay
As ice-storms do. Often you must have seen them
Loaded with ice a sunny winter morning
After a rain. They click upon themselves
As the breeze rises, and turn many-colored
As the stir cracks and crazes their enamel.
Soon the sun's warmth makes them shed crystal shells
Shattering and avalanching on the snow-crust—

Frost first influenced Meredith as a young man, and Meredith's undergraduate senior thesis (1940) was on Frost. Despite Frost's fame, Meredith's *An Analysis of the Poetic Method of Robert Frost*, was "one of the first essays to analyze Frost's poetry." In it we see some ideas that will manifest themselves later in Meredith's work. He takes Frost's "Everything is as good as it is dramatic," and reasons that clearly defined characters in vividly described settings will enhance the narrative tension in a poem and engage the reader. He also surmises from his analysis that "Frost places the burden of interpretation on the reader while simultaneously indicating his intended meaning," (most of Meredith's work does this, but not all, given the many explanatory notations he offered in some of his works), and that other Frost beliefs helped mold his "initial perceptions of poetry and its role in society."[26]

They met in person when Meredith began teaching at the Bread Loaf Writers' Conference (1958-1962), became friends, and remained friends for the rest of their lives. Meredith even accompanied Frost on a reading tour in 1960.[27] Meredith said of his time with Frost, "I feel that was one of the great instructions of my life, just to hang around and watch how he took things, his absolute solidity in the face of the twentieth century that he never made. I think that's one of the things that I've learned—that poems have to be one's own identity."[28]

He credits Frost with "making me, in my own way, strive for the kind of colloquial language that distinguishes his poems. I see a decline in the borrowed rhetoric of my first book, and gradually my poems begin to sound more and more like me—sometimes to the point of blank dullness, but anyhow they're my own. I learned that from his poems…And I

---

[26] Unknown. "Senior Honors Thesis, Princeton, 1940. "An Analysis of the Poetic Method of Robert Frost"." Web. <http://collections.conncoll.edu/meredith/works/thesis/>. Retrieved 20 July 18.

[27] Rotella, Guy L. Three Contemporary Poets of New England : William Meredith, Philip Booth, and Peter Davison. Boston : Twayne Publishers, 1983. Print. Twayne's United States Authors Series ; TUSAS 437; Twayne's United States Authors Series ; TUSAS 437. p.7

[28] Gerald, Gregory Fitz, et al. "The Frost Tradition: A Conversation with William Meredith." *Southwest Review*, vol. 57, no. 2, 1972, p. 114.

learned from him how to find poems, to stalk them."[29] Elsewhere Meredith notes how in writing "In Memory of Robert Frost" he said he 'knocked out a lot of carefully rhymed iambic pentameter and tried for flatness of tone," so again we see a deliberate divergence from his preferred inclination. [30]

Here, he again subordinates his own work, but clearly feels indebted to Frost for the lessons. Frost also helped with his attempts to "keep a sense of humor always at the corner of the picture," but he equally credits "Auden's phrase for the artist, *homo ludens*, man playing," as an inspiration to retain humor in his work and outlook on life. This comes from Auden's 1962 much read and referenced collection of essays *The Dyer's Hand,* but Auden most likely got the idea and expression from Dutch historian Johan Huizinga's 1938 book *Homo Ludens*. Perhaps this is another example of the hard-to-detect threads of literary influence across time.

Meredith directly attributes "Walter Jenks' Bath" (originally appearing in The New Yorker, June 8, 1968) as a "critical gift from Frost, a poem his critical insight had enabled me to find."[31] The gift was advice to get himself, the poet, out of the way and so Meredith "gave the poem away. I gave it to a fourteen-year-old high-school student, approximately one-third my then age." He made the teenager black and a resident of a town in Wisconsin Meredith had only spent one night in while passing through (Meredith's initiative with founding the Upward Bound program at Connecticut College and his involvement with it from 1964-1968 (the year "Walter Jenks' Bath" was published in *The New Yorker)* likely

---

[29] Gerald, Gregory Fitz, et al. "The Frost Tradition: A Conversation with William Meredith." *Southwest Review*, vol. 57, no. 2, 1972, p. 115.
[30] Gerald, Gregory Fitz, et al. "The Frost Tradition: A Conversation with William Meredith." *Southwest Review*, vol. 57, no. 2, 1972, p. 113
[31] Reasons for Poetry and The Reason for Criticism. Two Lectures Delivered at the Library of Congress on May 7, 1979 and May 5, 1980. Retrieved 27 July 2018.

also contributed to his creating a poem from a young African-American's perspective). What's also interesting is that this influence from Frost—gifting a poem to another persona—along with the success of Meredith's good friend John Berryman was having with his persona-based *Dreamsongs* collection, could very likely have contributed to Meredith's subsequent 1975 book, *Hazard the Painter,* being an entirely persona-based collection.

For Meredith, poetry was generally not a weapon to wield in a political cause (though certainly others were free to do so), but rather his "human concern, as a poet, requires me to look at and answer these political questions, but not necessarily to tell other people the answers and certainly not to write propaganda poems." He goes on with his always subtle humor to reinforce this belief, when he states "one has to do what's in character; don't for instance, think you can judge the excellence of a modern poet by his attendance record at anti-Vietnam rallies.[32] He said all of this publicly in 1972, but privately it seems political issues still took up some of his emotional and writing energy.

Despite this, he did say that during the Vietnam War his "political conscience" had him rethinking his naval vessel poems published after WW2 because "World War II was very much more plausible than any violence that this nation has been involved with since, to my mind." He was proud of what he and his countrymen did during their war, but poems like his "we probably won't have again because of what we've done to the sea and because of the promiscuous bloodiness of our wars."

In 1980's *The Cheer* he got around to publishing his 1969 poem "A Mild-Spoken Citizen Finally Writes to the White House" and "Nixon's the One" in 1975's *Hazard, the*

---

[32] Gerald, Gregory Fitz, et al. "The Frost Tradition: A Conversation with William Meredith." *Southwest Review*, vol. 57, no. 2, 1972, pp. 110.

Painter. In both of these the speaker is taking to task an America that has gone off the rails by a leader deemed unworthy of the office. So while none of his political poems are purely propaganda, as his moral compass and sense of manners would not allow him to do that, these poems are clearly release valves for his mind. We see a poet reflecting on a country diverging from the one he proudly served while in uniform, and a poetry commenting on a contemporary political issue.

But nearly 25 years earlier Meredith hit on a truth we writers and readers never seem to grasp and constantly have to re-learn regarding poetry and politics—every era can be seen as a turbulent time, "a time like this", particularly to those living in it. Even the Greeks and Romans had writers bemoaning the decline of current society and its leaders, and the approaching apocalypse—always just around the corner. In 1948's *Ships and Other Figures* "Envoi", he writes:

Go, little book. If anybody asks
Why I add poems to a time like this,
Tell how the comeliness I can't take in
Of ships and other figures of content
Compels me still until I give them names;
And how I give them names impatiently,
As who should pull up roses by the roots
That keep him turning on his empty bed,
The smell intolerable and thick with loss.

But despite each turbulent time, it is the duty of the poet to continue to still bring words to bear and art into the world. This is another gift poetry offers us to all—the same eternally repeated feelings and concerns brought to us freshly in the words of our time and the context of our culture, so we—the people of each age—can understand them. Meredith knew this, too. At a 1979 conference in Struga, he presented "The Language of Poetry In

Defense of Human Speech," [33] where only one of twenty-eight excellent points he made was:

> When I am writing a poem, in the State of Connecticut, in the United States of America, in 1979, I listen not only to the content of the poem but for words which the people of my time and place would hear as the most precise (and therefore delightful) expression of that content. My listening is deliberately local: a time, a place, a social ambiance. What I hope to hear is a voice, a dialect of the mind.

While he was raised Episcopalian, a practical, daily faith practice does not appear to have been a central part of most of his adult life, despite occasionally referencing faith or God in his work. Later in life he would fairly regularly give faith-tinged orations at his college's Chapel. In 1958's *The Open Sea* he writes, "Although not yet a man given to prayer, I pray / For each creature lost since the start of the sea, / And give thanks it was not I, nor yet one close to me." This poem is a precursor to *The Wreck of the Thresher*, and perhaps informs why that poem was so emotionally compelling a few years down the road. Note the first instance of the word "yet". It acknowledges the speaker's belief in God's involvement with man, a speaker unwilling to directly subordinate himself to a higher power at this particular time, but knowing he should/would at some point in life. These thoughts regarding God's involvement with us continued in his life. But maybe God speaks through people. "I suppose it seems to me that the priestly function of artists in a society is to administer spiritual vision," he said in 1983.[34]

One gets the sense the few overtly religious themed poems he wrote were done more as intellectual exercises or historical musings, and with an intellectual's undertone

---

[33] Meredith, William. "The Language of Poetry in Defense of Human Speech: Some Notes on the Topic of the Struga Symposium of 1979." *The American Poetry Review*, vol. 8, no. 6, 1979, pp. 14–15.

[34] Hirsch, Edward, and William Meredith. "The Art of Poetry XXXIV : William Meredith." *Paris review* (1985) Print. p.39

that perhaps formal religion does more harm than good but that it does have a place in civilized society.

For instance, "Notre Dame de Chartres" tells the story of a relic (the shirt worn by Mary, the mother of Jesus, at his birth) being spared in the fire that mostly destroys the church, but the speaker hints his faith is not the same as the true believers, who thought this a miracle. To the speaker, the miracle is "the faith that burned / Bright and erroneous / and built that house." To the speaker, the tenets are wrong, but the result, a beautiful gothic church in France, are right. The speaker refers to "the legend of God's mother," not Mary as divine vessel.

One thing I really liked about this poem though is the final line, where, after speaking the whole poem about the mother (Mary) of God (Jesus), the "father" finally enters the story. The shirt was saved only because the church (the "house") was made of stone, and it was "the stone that slept in the groin of France." God might not always be right, the speaker seems to say, but what beauty man has built in God's honor. And this church wasn't the only product of France to impress and impact Meredith's life and work.

When discussing the reason he translated Guillaume Apollinaire's *Alcools : Poems 1898-1913,* published in 1964, the same year *The Wreck of the Thresher*, Meredith begins and ends the discussion with the same thought, worded differently. He begins with "It may have to do with our needing to refresh the themes and images of our own poetry at this moment," and ends with "because those poems [*Alcools*] not only had enormous excitement for people of our moment, but they also, I think, were very useful for me. I don't believe any poet gets involved with a translation that doesn't have something to do with where's he's going, too."[35] Meredith found something he needed in Apollinaire and dove in. Steegmuller noted that "All of *Alcools* is particularly interesting because in it we witness the actual birth of a new poetry." So where was Meredith going at that time?

Well, keep in mind, he had always stayed true to order and traditional forms as a guiding principle— "my formal proclivity" he called it. "If there is a certain excess of formality in my poetry, it's because the poems that move me most deeply were from a more decorous period of American poetry."[36] I would add that is not just the more "decorous" periods and styles of American poetry, but also those of the poets across the pond. In discussing his translation of Apollinaire's "Autumn Crocuses", Meredith notes, "I have been influenced by the sonnet-like original version of this poem. A skilled reader of the French would have no trouble reconstructing anapaestic tetrameter lines, irregularly rhymed."[37] He knew formal poetry instinctively, and had to strive consciously to not create such. This "proclivity" was ingrained in his nature and his training.

Perhaps by this point in his career, he was feeling stilted, restrained. In an undated interview for *Poetry Miscellany*, a copy provided by the interviewer, poet Richard Jackson, and published sometime in the 1980's, Meredith mentioned "I felt formal prosody was chaining me, that I was playing it safe behind rhyme and meters." Seeing the success some of the wilder and looser poets of his day were having, he couldn't quite admit to modeling them, the antithesis of who he thought himself to be, but he could again go to his "elders"—in this case, Apollinaire—for guidance and inspirations, while still maintaining

---

[35] Gerald, Gregory Fitz, et al. "The Frost Tradition: A Conversation with William Meredith." *Southwest Review*, vol. 57, no. 2, 1972, pp. 112.
[36] Gerald, Gregory Fitz, et al. "The Frost Tradition: A Conversation with William Meredith." *Southwest Review*, vol. 57, no. 2, 1972, pp. 116.
[37] Apollinaire, Guillaume, and Francis Steegmuller. *Alcools : Poems, 1898-1913*. Translated by William Meredith, First ed., Doubleday & Company, 1964. p. 226.

an academic and intelligent sheen to his work. "Apollinaire's was one of the first really open imaginations in poetry, or so I think. And I have one of the up-tightest imaginations in modern poetry, or so I think. So I realized this was an affinity I had found that would be good for me to explore. I wrote some poems when I was working on Apollinaire that started me in a whole new direction." [38]

Meredith published hundreds of poems over the course of his career, in a wide variety of styles, all of which contributed to him developing his own intelligent and accessible verse. But he knew his style wasn't the only style, and that advocating for poetry as a whole is how it would become appealing to more practitioners and readers. In two lectures delivered at the Library of Congress one year apart during his tenure as Consultant in Poetry, Meredith eloquently argued for a "more generous definition of poetry" and for a "similar generosity of spirit among the critics." To support his positions he quotes Eliot, Ashberry, Auden, Pinsky, Hass, Frost, Zbigniew Herbert, Rilke, June Jordan, and Jarrell (who also quotes Whitman and Tennyson). All of these other writers informed his beliefs about the role of poetry in our society and helped to propel him towards and sustain him as our country's top-positional-poet. [39]

Years earlier, in a May 1966 he had already crystalized his beliefs about the role of art in our society and in our education programs. In response to the Princeton Chairman's article on the future of "the creative arts at Princeton," Meredith defends the creative arts at Princeton and discusses the differences between the scholar and the artist:

Creative activities are being used by today's students in a somewhat new

---

[38] Gerald, Gregory Fitz, et al. "The Frost Tradition: A Conversation with William Meredith." *Southwest Review*, vol. 57, no. 2, 1972, pp. 112
[39] Reasons for Poetry and The Reason for Criticism. Two Lectures Delivered at the Library of Congress on May 7, 1979 and May 5, 1980. Retrieved 27 July 2018.

way: to explore their most serious beliefs and feelings. Art can accommodate the complexity of their world more flexibly than the subjects they are studying, on the one hand, or the very limited roll they are allowed to play in their society, on the other…Scholarship is an act of orderly enquiry. The creative discipline is much more radical: it is frequently obliged to be controversial, individual, rancorous, destructive. Scholarship can be taught and graded, with rough justice and occasional injustice. Art, in its own time, cannot. [40]

My brief study of William Meredith has shown me the proof of these last two sentences, and that direct influence can be discovered, attributed, and acknowledged (by the poet, critics, and scholars), and that there will also always be environmental/circumstantial influences at work on a poet, some more discernable than others. Poets evolve over time, as does our concept of poetry, and being open to both changes allows the poet and readers to grow, and poetry to evolve with the times. It is a continuous circular process.

Meredith was formally trained by and informally mentored by some of the best poets of his day; he sought guidance from the poets who came before him and offered him the opportunity to share in an orderly poetry experience early in his career as he preferred, experimented away from, but ultimately returned.

However, my biggest takeaway from this short study is this: it is our tendency to put poets into categories and compare them with other writers, previous and contemporary, as an aid to try and help us grasp their work. But in studying Meredith's works and his writings about other poets and their poems, I was struck by the realization that perhaps we do not always imitate writers who've come before us—often we will not have encountered them by the time we write something similar—but rather as we progress in our study of earlier poets, we recognize the affinity of our earlier work with theirs—their habitual

---

[40] *Daily Princetonian*, Volume 90, Number 21, March 3, 1966, retrieved 27 July 2018

subjects, voice, style of writing, etc.—and begin to develop the language to describe our similarities to them and advocate our appreciation for our poetic forebears. It is this "language of the tribe" that Meredith so often referenced in interviews that he has helped me begin to develop by letting me borrow his eyes for a while.

Works Cited

Apollinaire, Guillaume, William Meredith, and Francis Steegmuller. *Alcools : Poems, 1898-1913*. First edition. ed. Garden City, N.Y.: Doubleday & Company, Inc., 1964. Print.

Bradley, James. *Flyboys : A True Story of Courage*. 1st ed. ed. Boston: Little, Brown and Co., 2003. Print.

Collier, William. ""Eulogy for William Meredith."" (2007)

Gerald, Gregory Fitz, Paul Ferguson, and William Meredith. "The Frost Tradition: A Conversation with William Meredith." *Southwest Review* 57.2 (1972): 108-117. Print.

Gregerson, Linda. "Book Review: Partial Accounts: New and Selected Poems." *Poetry* 151.5 (1988): 423-426. Print.

Harte, Jack. "*an Irishman's Diary: Jack Harte on William Meredith's Pilgrimage to Yeats's Sligo.*" *Irish Times,* 2015, Print.

Hirsch, Edward, and William Meredith. "The Art of Poetry XXXIV : William Meredith." *Paris review* (1985)Print.

Meredith, William. "Reasons for Poetry and The Reason for Criticism. Two Lectures Delivered at the Library of Congress on May 7, 1979 and May 5, 1980. Retreived 27 July 2018." Web. <https://www.loc.gov/item/91740998>.

Meredith, William, and Archibald MacLeish. *Love Letter from an Impossible Land.* New Haven: Yale University Press, 1944. Print. The Yale Series of Younger Poets, v. 42 .

Meredith, William. *Earth Walk: New and Selected Poems.* [1st ed.]. ed. New York: Knopf, 1970. Print. Borzoi Books .

---. *Effort at Speech : New and Selected Poems*. Evanston, Ill. : TriQuarterly Books/Northwestern University Press, 1997. Print.

---. *Hazard, the Painter : [Poems]*. 1st ed. ed. New York: Knopf, 1975. Print.

Meredith, William. "The Language of Poetry in Defense of Human Speech: Some Notes on the Topic of the Struga Symposium of 1979." *The American Poetry Review* 8.6 (1979): 14-15. Print.

Meredith, William. *Partial Accounts : New and Selected Poems*. 1st ed. ed. New York, N.Y.: Knopf, 1987. Print.

---. *Poems are Hard to Read*. Ann Arbor: University of Michigan Press, 1990. Print. Poets on Poetry .

---. *Ships and Other Figures. [Poems]*. [Princeton]: Pub. for the Princeton Univ. Library by Princeton Univ. Press, 1948. Print.

---. *The Wreck of the Thresher, and Other Poems.* [1st ed.]. ed. New York: Knopf, 1964. Print.

Rotella, Guy L. *Three Contemporary Poets of New England : William Meredith, Philip Booth, and Peter Davison.* Boston : Twayne Publishers, 1983. Print. Twayne's United States Authors Series ; TUSAS 437; Twayne's United States Authors Series ; TUSAS 437.

Unknown. "Senior Honors Thesis, Princeton, 1940. "An Analysis of the Poetic Method of Robert Frost"." Web. <http://collections.conncoll.edu/meredith/works/thesis/>.

Young, Vernon. "Poetry Chronicle: The Light is Dark enough." *The Hudson Review* 34.1 (1981): 141-154. Print.

THE LANGUAGE OF THE TRIBE: WILLIAM MEREDITH & ROBERT LOWELL'S LAST DINNER TOGETHER

By Michael Collier

Before I read any of William Meredith's poems, I read this: "Meredith is an expert writer and knows how to make his meters and sentences accomplish hard labors. His intelligent poems, unlike most poems, have a character behind them." That's what Robert Lowell wrote about Meredith's third book, *The Open Sea* (1958), and it was used as jacket copy in 1970 for *Earth Walk*, Meredith's new and selected poems. If I was uncertain about what Lowell meant by character, I didn't have to look very far to find out. In a short foreword to *Earth Walk*, Meredith says, "An author's chronological account of his work, like the selected poems here, insinuates an autobiography or at least a character that he would like the reader to accept: that of a candid man paying scrupulous attention to the events of his life." And a few sentences, later, "To say that a man's poems are honest is to say more about the terms of poetry than about the man." I liked the idea that a poem could be honest, more honest than the person who wrote it, and yet the poem might have the effect of making honesty the poet's goal. I thought of honesty as a form of truth— and at eighteen, which was my age at the time, I wanted to speak truth; but also at that age, I believed truth was something you felt and declared rather than noticed and made, that honesty was intrinsic rather than hard-won.

In his essay, "In Loving Memory of the Late Author of Dream Songs," Meredith, writing about the time he spent accompanying John Berryman to Goddard College in 1971, a few months before Berryman killed himself, recalled the yearning the two had for "decorum and even old-fashioned manners." Meredith wasn't speaking about manners as "social behavior," of which he characterized their own as "dubious," but rather as a "social ideal." He saw manners in the same way he saw literary form: as "an agreed-on language, an established position from which you could negotiate with accuracy toward or away from human intimacy." Meredith's discussion of manners and decorum lead him to make a distinction between two kinds of honesty. One was "promiscuous honesty" that was "preferred to conventional manners," which he saw everywhere in the culture of the 1960s and 70s. "Promiscuous honesty" entailed "an evasion of the social predicament" and pretended "to candor." The other form of honesty recognized "that all honest engagements are negotiations…that require the expense of attention."

In "Morning after Dining with a Friend," a poem from Robert Lowell's last book, *Day by Day* (1977), published just before his death, he describes his first encounter with Meredith, in 1955:

> I met you first at the old Met Opera Club, shy,
> correct, in uniform,
>
> your regulation on active duty substitute for
>
> black tie—
>
> Poet and aviator at
>
> 36,
> the eternal autumn of youth.

Meredith had been a pilot in both the Army Air Corps and the Navy during World War II and after the war went into the reserves before he was called up for duty in Korea, in which he served as a Navy carrier pilot. Meredith liked flying, and as a gay man he liked the company of men, but he also felt compelled to continue to serve his country. Of that generation of poets who served in the military in WWII, I can't think of another who still would have been on active duty in 1955, two years after the end of the Korean War. In the same way that he believed in a social ideal of manners and decorum, he believed in ideal forms of citizenship. Serving one's country in the military was a way of negotiating honestly with the obligations of citizenship. This didn't mean that he believed military service was the only way to negotiate those obligations, but rather that it was the way he felt compelled to respond, given his character and temperament, just as it was in Lowell's character to fulfill his obligation as a citizen during WWII in jail, as a "fire-breathing Catholic C.O."

Even in the rarified world of the Metropolitan Opera Club of the 1950s, Meredith substituting a military uniform for black-tie, which of course is just another sort of uniform, would have set him apart, would have made clear that he wanted to be taken not only as a "poet and aviator" but as a cultivated officer and gentleman. And yet Lowell, in his poem, sees through Meredith's presentation of self to that essence of his character that is both "shy" and "correct." Those two words crucially bring the meeting to life, and through them Lowell negotiates the encounter in an act of "scrupulous attention" or rather at the "expense of attention."

> As if to prove how difficult it is to sustain attentive honesty—or perhaps how little you need to establish it—Lowell's description of Meredith as "the eternal autumn of youth," five lines later, has the feel of mere representation. What Lowell calls an "image" at the start of the next stanza takes up the real occasion for the poem: a meeting they had, their last, in March of 1976, in Cambridge and Boston. Lowell sets the scene:

Waking wifeless is now a habit—
hearing the human-abstract rush of traffic, another
night, another day

entertaining nothing but my thoughts— Why
have I twisted your kind words and tortured
myself till morning?

My brain keeps flashing back last night— a booth
in the Greek restaurant,
now fronting the Boston Combat Zone— "We'd
be mad not to take a taxi back."

"I think Frost liked me better but
found you more amusing."

In the twenty or so intervening years since their first meeting, Lowell and Meredith had become good friends. In 1975, as a student of Meredith's at Connecticut College, I was invited to drive with him to Cambridge to hear Lowell read at Harvard. Lowell wasn't expecting to see Meredith that night, but when he saw him standing (I can't help now but think "shy" and "correct") in the outer ring of friends and well-wishers after the reading, Lowell lit up with pleasure and immediately made his way to greet him as well as to suggest he come to a party afterwards. What I witnessed in Lowell was a moment of genuine warmth and affection, almost of surprise and relief at having discovered a path to intimacy in an otherwise public event. If I hadn't already observed Meredith's interactions with others with whom he shared deep, long friendships (such as Muriel Rukeyser, Robert Penn Warren, and Richard Wilbur) I would have said Meredith's own reaction to Lowell that night had been reserved or even deferential rather than a manifestation of the quiet way he had of soliciting a response with a gentle, calm rectitude—a formal welcoming that offered a serious, principled smile. For Meredith, any human interaction was an opportunity for an honest encounter, not to be squandered, and yet there was nothing dour or morally pinched about it. In the two-and-a-half years that I had been Meredith's student, and then in the several before he had a catastrophic stroke, in 1983—and even in the decades beyond until he died, in 2007—I spent many hours in his company and I can't remember ever having had a trivial conversation with him. It's not that you couldn't talk about trivial things, but he had a way of finding in small talk larger concerns.

Lowell died on September 12, 1977, not long after Helen Vendler reviewed *Day by Day* in the August 14 *New York Times*, ahead of its official publication date. "Morning after Dining with a Friend" had been written after Lowell had sent Meredith a series of poems that would appear in *Day by Day*. These poems became one of the topics of conversation the night of their meal at the Greek restaurant. Meredith was under no illusion about his gifts as a poet compared with Lowell's. In fact, he liked to say of himself that he was a B+ poet, a characterization that always made me, and other friends, uncomfortable. Even if it carried some truth when he compared himself to Lowell, it made for a rare awkwardness. I never knew quite how to respond. Was Meredith wanting me to reassure him that in fact he was better than B+? Was I supposed to admire his honesty? It also made me aware, as Lowell's poem does ("I think Frost liked me better / but found you more amusing") that friendship aside, Meredith was always aware of the literary pecking order. I mention this not to point out a flaw or contradiction in Meredith's character— although why not? —but rather to show how manners and decorum, if they're worth anything, are in tension with the social ideal they imagine. In other words, manners and decorum could miss their mark, so to speak, but that didn't mean they were false or artificial. Instead, like everything else that has to do with human relationships, they were complicated and imperfect.

In his essay, "Remembering Robert Lowell," Meredith gives his own account of their dinner and final meeting. Written within a few months of Lowell's death, the essay uses the occasion of their last meeting to describe their friendship. Some time had passed since they had seen each other, and Lowell, Meredith reports, lamented, "Our not getting together yearly is unnatural, isn't it?" Meredith tells us that he had not "heard much about the new book [*Day by Day*]" but had been shown "some revised and written-over poems from…the 'Ulysses and Circe' series." He also says that Lowell did not make mention of the changes occurring in his marriage to Caroline Blackwood. "We were not suddenly that intimate," Meredith writes, noting that "after almost two years; the friendship had suffered disuse, and that matter was private." Nevertheless, Lowell did tell him about a recent hospitalization at McLean's, which Meredith recalled as being for "tests in preparation for a new treatment." The tests also revealed Lowell had suffered recently from a mild heart attack, a harbinger of his death.

The fact that they had not seen each another for a few years is the likely reason for Lowell's poignant description of Meredith—no longer "the eternal autumn of youth"—that leads to the end of "Morning after Dining with a Friend." Lowell writes:

> That image has gained body: yet
> shrinks back this morning to its
> greener Platonic shade, the man of
> iron—
>
> not drinking, terrified of
> losing   your   mind…
> turning to me, calm
> by a triumph of impersonation:
>
> "if you could come a little nearer the
> language of the tribe."

Meredith remembers that at one point coming back from the men's room and passing through a "long, empty space of half-light," Lowell remarked, "It seems strange to see you with white hair." Of course, the unspoken conversation Lowell was having with himself was as much about his own preoccupation with aging as it was with his friend's, a preoccupation that is everywhere present in the poems he was writing at the time. Meredith had also confided to Lowell—his way of being intimate—that he had stopped drinking and was "terrified / of losing [his] mind." During the night, Lowell not only twists his friend's words but is haunted by the recognition they are both getting old. In the morning, however, the "image" of a white-haired Meredith, "shrinks back… / to its greener Platonic shade." The epithet Lowell finds for his friend, "the man of iron," gives corporeal substance to the metaphor of "Platonic shade" and has the effect of slightly mythologizing Meredith. But I think the epithet also cuts in a different direction, less positive, and anticipates the penultimate stanza, which asks us to consider that the "man of iron" is a façade.

Meredith had not seen "Morning after Dining with a Friend" until it was published in *Day by Day*—and, actually, I believe I brought the existence of the poem to his attention. Although Lowell did not identify who the friend was, the details left little room for doubt. Also, I was certain it was Meredith because I had heard him frequently talk about the "language of the tribe" in the classroom and in conversation, elsewhere. "The language of the tribe" is a notion Meredith adapted from T.S. Eliot's incorporation of Mallarmé's line (*"Donner un sens plus pur aux mots de la tribu"*) in "Little Gidding," which Eliot renders as "To purify the dialect of the tribe." For Meredith, however, the purified dialect of the tribe was not to be found in Eliot or Mallarmé but rather in the very American idiom of Robert Frost. Frost, on whom Meredith wrote his undergraduate thesis, composed in a colloquial American idiom based on speech patterns. Meredith believed that poetry should be accessible to any moderately educated person. He also felt it should be useful and be a source of delight in our lives. The language of the tribe was the key to both accessibility and usefulness.

In his remembrance of Lowell, Meredith describes the usual part he played in their relationship as writers, one in which he frequently asked questions about "places where [Lowell's] poems were unclear: where the reader was not told clearly what the poem was saying (rather than what it meant)." This was a role that began in 1969 when the two poets were together in Madrid. While there, proofs of Lowell's first *Notebook* arrived from the publisher and needed to be corrected. Meredith recalls how many of the last- minute changes Lowell made were the result of his convincing Lowell to "clarify passages…that were not clear, not located in the poem as they were in his experience." Meredith had long believed that Lowell's poems "made severer demands on their readers than they needed to," a belief that was in keeping with his assessment "that many modern poets neglect the vulgar energy of speech for a literary language of their own." Because Meredith had seen only a few "revised and written-over poems" from *Day by Day*, he did not have a better sense of how much nearer Lowell had in fact moved to the language of the tribe, as Meredith conceived it. Nevertheless, from the little he'd seen, he "found [the poems] more accessible" and told Lowell before they left Dunster House for the Greek restaurant that "his language was moving nearer to the language of the tribe." Meredith's comment sounds descriptive rather than proscriptive, which is how Lowell must have heard it or thought he heard it, and as such it had carried the ring of a pronouncement that perhaps became the source of Lowell's self-torture.

After dinner, Meredith drove them back to Dunster House, where Lowell inscribed a copy of his *Selected Poems*. The inscription reveals that he was already turning over and worrying his old friend's remark. At first, Lowell inscribes, "One's books moving n…," but then he strikes it out and replaces it with, "One's language moving nearer the language…." The slip, if that's what it was, is interesting and revealing. By substituting "books" for "language," and language was without question the word Meredith would have used, Lowell has in mind the literary artifact that language produces rather than the human fabric and connective tribal tissue Meredith had in mind. "Books" indicates a moment of inattentiveness that Lowell recognizes and quickly corrects. The dedication page with its hesitant, revised inscription is a metaphor, an accurate and graphic symbol of Lowell's life and art, which was writ large with revision. As Lowell adjusts and revises his inscription so that it comports more closely with Meredith's actual words, he literally enacts(inscribes) in front of his friend, and on the page, the direction his friend wants Lowell's poems to take—"to move nearer the language of the tribe."

We might think the revised inscription, which includes, Meredith tells us, "a phrase still undeciphered" and is signed, "Love, Cal," might be the end of the episode, but it is in fact something like a mid-point. "Morning after Dining with a Friend," begins with Lowell opining that "[w]aking wifeless is now a habit." It's easy to imagine him adrift in bed, "entertaining," he tells us, "nothing but his thoughts" as he listens to the "human-abstract rush of traffic" coming from Memorial Drive along the Charles. In this abandoned, slightly self-pitying state, he asks, "Why have I twisted your kind words / and tortured myself till morning?" While it's possible the only kind words Lowell twisted were the ones Meredith used about the language of the tribe, it's likely there were other aspects of the evening that made Lowell's night fitful and self-recriminating. The poem carries with it a parenthetical marker or subtitle "(Some weeks after Logan Airport)" which refers to "Logan Airport, Boston," the opening poem of the second section in part III of *Day by Day*, dedicated to his wife. Another poem, "Suburban Surf," with its parenthetical "(After Caroline's return)" closes the section. The first poem laments Blackwood's departure, while the second marks her return. In between these poems, Lowell has placed "Morning after Dining with a Friend." In the poem about Blackwood's departure, Lowell is preoccupied with the hardening of "mannerisms" that take place in people and in relationships over time, as well as the unrelenting process of aging. "I cannot bring back youth with the snap of my belt," he writes in "Logan Airport, Boston." And further, he asks, "Is it cynical to deliquesce, / as Adam did in age, / though outwardly goldleaf, / true metal, and make-up?" (No wonder, he was struck by the dissonance of seeing Meredith's white hair.) In "Suburban Surf," Lowell is awake in bed listening to the surf of morning traffic, but now he's holding his wife in his "insomniac arms." When she wakes, he says she is "like a bear tipping a hive for honey," shaking "the pillow for French cigarettes." What follows—"No conversation"—reminds us of the hardened mannerisms of "Logan Airport, Boston" and Blackwood's departure, and so Lowell turns his attention to the traffic and finds in its "whooshing waves," its "mechanical— / soothe, delay, divert," a kind of "truce with uncertain heaven." After which, he makes this assertion, "A false calm is the best calm." Or is it really a question he's been asking himself, one that he carried over from his dinner with Meredith?

Perhaps the most powerful lines in "Morning after Dining with a Friend" occur after Meredith reveals his terror over losing his mind. At that point, Lowell tells us, Meredith turned to him "calm / by a triumph of impersonation." Similarly to "man of iron," the line "a triumph of impersonation" contains ambiguity. It's not clear to me if Lowell trusts Meredith's "calm" demeanor or if he finds in his "triumph of impersonation" an achievement to admire. A poet I know, who is a scholar of Lowell's work, told me "Lowell's depiction of Meredith is harsh, typically harsh." Harsh might be one way to read this part of the poem, but given Lowell's strategic placement of it in *Day by Day* and the way it's framed and refers to Blackwood's going and coming, it seems more likely that Lowell found in his encounter with Meredith a powerful and perhaps rueful confirmation of his own preoccupations.

If Lowell found himself wondering the next morning why he had twisted his friend's kind words, Meredith found himself puzzling over the revised and partially undeciphered inscription. In his remembrance of Lowell, Meredith writes: "Before I saw 'Morning after Dining with a Friend,' but after I had pondered the inscription, I wrote a poem in his memory containing this line: 'Your language moved slowly towards our language.'" Here the impulse is clearly descriptive, and it counters, without foreknowledge, Lowell's memory of what was said: "If you could *come* a little nearer / the language of the tribe" (my italics). Meredith's remark about Lowell's new work, he offers, "was intended as praise," and he believed Lowell understood it as such, even though Lowell's poem "would suggest something more ambivalent on one or both sides." Although Meredith was given to say that Lowell was his "better," he wasn't going to have his friend put words in his mouth. Nor was he going to give Lowell a pass because he had died. Nevertheless, his remembrance also demonstrates that he understood the responsibility he had to be as fair as possible in his recollection of their last meeting because Lowell could offer no response. Generosity, which was a natural part of Meredith's character, demanded that he assign a portion of blame to himself for their misunderstanding. He writes, "I meant…to say" to Lowell "that I was glad that the new poems seemed nearer to the density and energy of common verbal experience"; and then he speculates, again generously, about what might have happened during the night that caused Lowell to twist his words. Meredith suggests that Lowell was so used to having his friend ask him questions about his poems that during the night Lowell rephrased Meredith's remark "as a question, and that he attributed that question about his language to me, who had asked him so many." Perhaps there is no better illustration of what Lowell meant by the character behind Meredith's poems than his attempt at an honest and balanced appraisal of what took place between them that night. It provides a model for how to negotiate a disagreement with a friend in public, and, more delicately, with a friend who is dead.

Lowell's twisting of his friend's kind words was not the only kink of misquotation in "Morning after Dining with a Friend" that Meredith felt compelled to straighten. Another instance occurs when Lowell has Meredith say, "'I think Frost liked me better / but found you more amusing.'" "Amusing," Meredith writes, "is not a weighty word in my vocabulary, not a praise word, certainly not a word adequate to the felt disturbance of heart, dazzle of mind, that one experienced in Lowell's company." "Amusing" did not capture the "profound gaiety" Lowell exhibited as a "great mimic" and "a playful father." What Meredith remembers saying is, "I think Frost found you more interesting." In the same way he took a portion of responsibility for Lowell's misunderstanding his response to the new poems, Meredith admits, too, that what he "meant to say to him that night" was that he "envied him that [Lowell] could interest Frost more than [he] could have hoped to." To most readers, the difference between "amusing" and "interesting" might not seem crucial—but to Meredith, and this again speaks to his character, "amusing" was an insufficient word to carry the weight of what he was trying to say; and part of what he was trying to say was that he envied Lowell, which is not an attractive thing to admit, especially to a friend.

The generation of poets of which Meredith was a prominent member was not known for its optimism. Many of its poets led tragic and painful lives. It was also a generation greatly influenced by literary experiments and cultural upheaval that called into question and often denounced the traditions and conventions that had guided poets for centuries. Meredith's natural modesty—and his belief in manners and decorum as a reflection of an ideal for human interaction—called him not so much to stand against the upheaval but to offer an alternative. He had watched two of his poet friends, John Berryman and Robert Lowell, as they took themselves again and again to the "dark brink" of personal disaster. Their poems often enacted the drama of their perilous lives. Meredith understood that their art was an honest, hard-won, and accurate response to their experience. They were acting in character, just as he was when Lowell met him at the Metropolitan Opera Club. The alternative Meredith offered was in many ways unfashionable, as it still is today. I'm not talking about the style of his poems, because all styles eventually become unfashionable, and this is often especially true for much experimental writing. No, what was unfashionable then and now was the calm, equitable, reticent, scrupulous decorum of human interaction that his poems tried to enact. In his poem, "In Loving Memory of the Late Author of Dream Songs," Meredith writes, "I do what's in character, I look for things / to praise on the river banks and I praise them." While this statement sounds pretty straightforward, it's not. Listen to how the stanza preceding those lines will have complicated the meaning of praise:

> Morale is what I think about all the time
> now, what hopeful men and women can say and do.
> But having to speak for you, I can't lie. 'Let
> his giant faults appear, as sent
> together with his virtues down,' the song says.
> It says suicide is a crime
> and that wives and children deserve better than this. None of us
> deserved, of course, you.

Meredith finds a way to criticize and chide Berryman for his suicide, yet at the same time he weighs that against the poet's many "virtues" and the privilege of having had a friendship with him. Meredith takes his license for the poem by asserting his preoccupation with "morale." In another poem, "Hazard's Optimism," he tells us that Hazard, his superego, "is in charge of morale in a morbid time." Webster's defines morale as "the mental and emotional condition (as of enthusiasm, confidence, or loyalty) of an individual or group with regard to the function or tasks at hand." Meredith's formulation of the task, both of poetry and life, is to discover "what hopeful men and women can say and do."

This is in keeping with Meredith's belief that there are three fundamental stances poets and poems can take: dissident, apologist, or solitary. The dissident's underlying stance is that of social critic; the apologist's is "acceptance or approval of the human or social predicament of his tribe"; the solitary's is of the poem "talking to itself" with "no implicit agreement about social needs or predicaments." Although all three stances can be found in any single poet, and potentially all at once, Meredith thought by attraction, temperament, and circumstance, one of the stances was apt to prevail at any given time. For most of his life, Meredith assigned himself the stance of an apologist, not because he was against political dissent (take a look at his poems "Nixon's the One" and "A Mild-Spoken Citizen Finally Writes to the White House"); and not because his poems couldn't strike a solitary's pose (take a look at "Country Stars" and "Ideogram"); but because by temperament he believed the task at hand was to boost the morale of the tribe—and one of the ways to do this was to defend and keep alive social manners and aesthetic forms that remained useful.

"Apologist" nowadays has lost its older meaning of someone who defends a set of beliefs and has become a synonym for someone who often excuses the inexcusable. Meredith was fiercely not that kind of apologist. He was an optimist. The energy of the optimism that comes through his poems was his life's work, and late in his career, his mission was to celebrate the best aspects of humanity and the human spirit. His optimism was progressive and inclusive—and the decorum that guided it was fueled by a desire to find "the right words," as he says in "The Cheer." Like Hazard, Meredith was "[g]nawed by a vision of rightness /that no one else seems to see." What this vision required of him was to "bear witness" to "the shaped things he's seen— / a few things made by men, / a galaxy made well." Lowell may have found a willfulness in Meredith's optimism and his resolve to put a good face on the human predicament, a phrase Meredith liked to use. Perhaps this is why he perceived his friend's calm as a "false calm," arrived at "by a triumph of impersonation." I believe that Meredith's optimism was an honest expression of who he was, a "hopeful" man, and it was crucial for his art to reflect that, which it did.

I can't think of any poet of his generation or in the generations since who would risk titling a book of poems *The Cheer*, and yet that's what Meredith called his last book, published in 1980, a few years before a stroke took away his ability to write poems. The risk, of course, is that readers accustomed to Lowell's self-described "lurid, rapid, garish, grouped, / heightened from life, / yet paralyzed by fact" "snapshot[s]" might find a cheeriness in cheer—but that's not what Meredith offered. He offered a way for us to access the optimism he believed was inherent in words. "Cheer or courage," he writes, "is what [the right words] are all born in." This is the profoundly comforting message that words and language carry, and as such they ask to embody their native cheer and courage, "even," as Meredith concludes his poem "The Cheer," "when it seems quite impossible to do." By suggesting to Lowell that his work had begun to move nearer the language of the tribe, he was suggesting it was coming closer to inhabiting the native optimism words contain. For Meredith, this was one of poetry's imperatives. To recognize it was a form of praise, and to be calm in that recognition, especially in the terrifying face of one's own decline, was not an impersonation but an assertion of character.

(This essay was written to honor the centenary of William Meredith's birth.)

Enabling Love

A
Tribute
To
William Meredith

By Tom Kirlin

Winner of the 2019 William Meredith Award in Poetry

Poets' Choice

A Major Work

Poems are hard to
read Pictures are hard
to see Music is hard
to hear
And people are hard to love

But whether from brute
need Or divine energy
At last mind eye and ear
And the great sloth heart will move.

                -William Meredith

Table of Contents

Foreword		7
I.	You Move Among Us	9
II.	The Literate Imagination	19
III.	It Was May	29
IV.	The End of Deception	41
V.	Self-Reckoning	51
VI.	The Center Cannot Hold	65
VII.	Efforts at Speech	73
VIII.	Impartial Laughter	83
Epilogue		89
Examples of Created Systems		93
Artist's Biography		97
Author's Biography		99

Acknowledgements

William Meredith, *Partial Accounts: New and Selected Poems*, Alfred A. Knopf (New York, 1987)

"Why the Soul Loves Catfish," Tom Kirlin, *Under the Potato Moon*, Little Red Tree Publishing, LLC (New London, 2013)

I
You Move Among Us

"A poet penetrates a dark disguise
After his own conception, little or large.
Crossing the scaleless asia of trouble
Where it seems no one could give himself
away, He gives himself away, he sets a scale."

A Korean Woman Seated By A Wall

Tom Kirlin   *You Move Among*

                              March

       or April

                              there
                              will be

                      FROST

                 p a r a d e s

                                   complaint

                  s a

                              f
                                        a
                              O
                                        t

            of

                 buck-
                              naked

                                             [poetic

                                        ] dreams

            HOWLing up
                       Kitemaug
                              Road

                  as
                       a

                                        C h i l l

            brick   WiND

cuts   its
   sharp   teeth

EnablingLove　　　　　　　　　　　　　　　　　　　Tom Kirlin

　　　　　　　　on the
　　　　　　　　TANgle
　　　　　　　　d

　　　　　　　　　　INNARDS

　　　　　　　of "We the　　　People"

　　　　for OH!　　You

　　　　　　　　　　& Far

　　　　　　　　　　　　　　too
Many
　　　　　　　　　　　　　　　　　Poets

LONGsin
　ce　　　　　　　　　　lie
　　　　　　buried

　in

　　p
　　a
　　r
　　a
　　d
　　s
　　e
　　　　　　　(Wyoming)
　　　　　　　　.

    Yes you,

           Sir William,

                        you & your

Astringent

Sweetwater

              WORDs

Tom Kirlin   *You Move Among Us*

                    still wet
                        my
                            whistle

                &

                        warm   Cheeks
                        m
                        our
Your poems
                    as
                            Fierce
    as
                            any
                            Flee
                            t of
                            20m Century
                            Poems

    for
                        You
                            set

                                Ablaz.e
                        the
                            brute Heart

                and Named
                                (our divine)
                                    needs.

            Indeed::   t deep
                            Your
                                Flight

deep   inside

the Psyche

Enabling Tom Kirlin
Love

        EXPLODES

    inside a Reader,

      FORcing

        U.S.
                to   EXamine

each Day
                (more)
     Honestly, Freely

    (& for)
           whatever reason

WHATEVE   we   wish
R   to   become

             it   will
             no   be
             t
                  easy
                  .

HOVERing

  now (slightly) beside

     VIGIL
     -ilam

     ENDurin
                words
    g you

    keep   (somewhat)

Tom Kirlin　　　　　　　　　　　　　*You Move Among Us*

LO O
　a　　　f

Your　AIR　borne　Legacy
　　　　　　　　re ceding

　　　　　　　　　though not completely

　　for who can
　　forget　　　　　　you

　　Received

　　　　　　　　the PULITZER Prize

Are recognized　　by

　　　　　The Academy of American

　Poets The Poetry Foundation

　　　　　　　　&
The ENTIRE

　　　　　　　　nation

　　　　　　of Bulgaria

　　　　　PLUS were
　　　　　　a Visiting Artist to
　Russia, India, Bulgria, Ireland,
　Greece.

　　　　　　　　　　　　Yet
　　the Norton
　　Anthology

dropped you
(recently)　　　　　You,

　　　　　a Cultured Voice,

Enabling Love Tom Kirlin

> not even mentioned
>   in the State Department's own

"American Poetry, 1945-1990: The Anti-

Tradition."

>   True:

> You are no
> Anti-Traditonalist!

> You

>   strafe   with
>   d us

> Sonnets   Villanelles

> Sestinas, etc.

>   (plus)

that   Constant RAPID

> Friendly

>   fire
>   of

>   p

P
O
R
C
U
P
i
N
E

rhymes

        hitting each mark
                in the wee dark

hours of our wine-soaked

                MORTALity.
That   you do/did
           so
(well; repeatedly)
            stands as

       TESTament
              t
 o   Your

own
            DIFFicult
                CHOices

                    as you seized & accept
CONsequenC
ES   disPLAYe
           d

Compassion (wit)   courage   duty

              Especially!
          in

       PARTIAL ACCOUNTS

(an Old Soul's war stories, told by its boyish KEEPer).

Yes, Sweet William, we COMMend and Thank You
            for
  (bringing into)   Being
a   more   Literate
    IMAGin ation.
  Now it is ours

to Keep.

II
The Literate Imagination

"The ocean was salt before we crawled to tears."
The Wreck Of The Thresher

Tom Kirlin   *The Literate Imagination*

Your craft   seldom
                    levitates/ radiates

                BEAUTY.

            No. Your Carrier ship/words
        dredge deeper, lifting

            s u b m e r e g e d

        Grief
(oh, how you yearn
for

                        land
                    for Trees!)

        mixing the body's   Wet

            Dirt with chaste hard

            Music

            so what I hear
                        is
    Anglo-Saxon
            words

            that you hang   like   a

            WREATH
                        of
    dry-eyed Love
                            around OUR
                (stiff)
            Necks,

and so encourage US

Enabling Love Tom Kirlin

to follow your

                Warrior   spirit

    into the ENDLESS

        Battle That is
Poetry (which turns stone)
                into
    flesh & being:

"Like that Greek boy whose name I now
forget Whose youth was one long study
to cut stone; One day his mallet
slipped...
So that the marble opened on a girl
Seated at music and wonderfully
fleshed And sinewed under linen,
riffling a harp; At which he knew
not that delight alone
The impatient muse intended, but, coupled with
it, grief- The harp-strings in particular were so
light-
And put his chisel down for marveling on that stone."
            A View of the Brookryn Bridge

You
chiseled   Away

  at your   Soul

        in so many ways,
knowin
g:

    "Poems are hard to
    read Pictures are hard
    to see Music is hard to

hear
And people are hard to love"
A Major [autobiographical] *Work*

And well before

your Craft

was half-grown, you poked about

                                                      life's
TRASHcans

                                    for bits of

half-NIBBLED

                            Humanity
-and when caught

                        like a Racoon

in the act, stood on your own two hind legs
and didn't back off.

    Your
            (animal)

                                 Instinct
for Survival   your Intellect
      Com
      mand ing

            our singular
                    Attention!!

            (precisely)
                          BEcause

    You   *so* unflinchingly   examine

        the dog in every
        Man.

    You stare at us
        looking

Enabling Love   Tom Kirlin

      Up   &

          D
          o
          w
          n

                    fearlessly

polishing the
Form   in your Heart
           our eyes, the souls

and   INVITE
        us   In
                demanding

    we too

        stAN

      D Straight

     Keep time

        and MEASure

as   Together   we

    Navigate
      the unmoored

    Past   Present
        &   Future.

And, EVER the
Raccoon,   You

    Slow-Dance

   with   words

Tom Kirlin *The Literate Imagination*

        Athletically   with Wit & Heart-felt

Compassion   as   if

        HOPing

to   trap

the
(half-   Conscience.
absent)

      Yes, as Muse, You

                    rap at our door
    Once Again,
           NEVER more

                tellingly
                than this,

      the 10•h year of your PASSing
         the 30•h ANNNERSARY

of
    Partial Accounts.

          Let us,
Kind
Reader,   therefore,

          CELEbrate:

Enabling Love   Tom Kirlin

"The Muse and Her Gentleman"

I.

Touched by illiterate longing, he was like the
man Who could lay a hand across her heart
And you might think this is because his
hand Was unfamiliar, but, truth is, she
Had never had a man who was a friend.

Now he is both afraid of what she is
And does, and interested because she says
she is A dancer at a downtown gentlemen's
club.

She could touch his arm, intimately,
Or not; he could send flowers, or flowery
words, To her hotel room, saying he is
coming, or not. He thinks he talks too
much, and is not beloved.

What do you call this awkward silence which stands
Now between dead poets, honest praise & us—
We the living, naked, afraid; they, humble revenants?
Aren't time & death sufficient
To meet the requirement of love?

IL

True rememberance is neither rich, nor poor
Nor orphaned, nor vain, nor ignorant. Death is well-
read; Remberance pensive, private, unsettled, awake,
irreverent Deep inside us. In death, true friendship
Becomes neither sleep nor sufficient.

Once among the living, William is become a Muse
–Your daughter, my son, a love among us for
words Borne well after high school graduation.

This morning, on-line, feeling orphaned, she
looks For empty space. His grave is full. My
page Undone. A wicked wink and her will is
one.
We write for less literate daughters and sons.

Still, she's touched. A tear runs, perhaps in
raccoon Sorrow. She looks hard at you–he at us
And laughs off these slight bumps, but not first
before Turning and sticking us with that wry,
untimely smile.

You, Sir William the Pen, will never
be "A fresh joint/ tossed into damp
sand."

III
It was May

"Itwas May
When things tend to look
allegorical."

Roots

Tom   *It Was May*
Kirlin

           How
                              did

                                        you

                     TRANSfor
                                        you rself
                     m from
Ariel
                              Warrior
                                                            to

                              (grou
                              nded)   Poet?

Clearly, you joined a Company:

                     Frost
Aude
n
Yeats
Lewis
Thomas
Robert Penn Warren
           Other Poets

                                                  who
           dined (daily) on
                                        NOTHING

                     but Harsh Truth. a

           Laughter and

                     (hard)

                              Consequences,

83

and

"Every last creature
Is the one it meant to be."
Consequences: ii. of love

Enabling Love Tom Kirlin

        HAUNTING
        lines

        that you applied
                  to yourself
as well as

      us
         (admittiing)

      you stole
          into FROSTs company

            with
            Lies

   (which)
   sometimes   are necessary

   to gain
          Admittance... no, rather
you
sought

        "respite from that blinding attention, [and]
     More likely, a friendship
     I felt I could only get by stealing."
               In Memory of Robert Frost

        Another
          of your poetic
Revelations
   is equally
   REVEALing:

"Whatever death is, it sets pretenders free."
                  For His Father

        which then is
Exceeded

        by these

l
i
n
e
s
:

Tom Kirlin   *It Was May*

                "I have been, except on one
occasion Myself. It is no good trying to be what
you are not.

We live among gangs who seem to have no stake
In what we're trying to do, no sense of property or
race, Yet if you speak with authority they will halt
and break And suddenly, one by one, show you a
local face."
                            Consequences: iii my acts

    Perhaps the
              Korea
             n
                     woma
made you do & say   n
it,
                                the one
        who wore a mask
        of such Suffering

that you,
    William the Aviator,

              u
        A   L
   v   T

       from your bomber's

Seat into Poetry & Teaching

            (LEAVing
            the AFFAIRS of War

                               to

                                          the Grim Reaper).

Enabling Love   Tom Kirlin

And while you SPARE
    us
        the   of
        Grimace   war,   of say,

Guernica,

          no
    doubt   somedays

    you leaned
        FORward
                behind your desk

& wondered
why   the Young

    seem *so* easily

Distracted

    AD miring

        the color of their socks
        & the size of their
Thighs,
many for-
    EVE
R

    Ignora
    nt that soldiers
    lost more than
        their

METriCAL
    feet.

So yes, I Take Heart

from your early Poetry, especially

Tom Kirlin *It Was May*

                your landing
                        of this Colliquy
                                with   your own

      budding Muse,

                Mrs. Leamington.

"Mrs. Leamington stood on a cloud
Quarreling with a dragon-it was May,
When things tend to look allegorical-
As I drove up the hill that silhouettes
Her house against the east. In any month She's
hard to place-scattered and sibylline: She
hangs the curtains for me in the fall (Rather
than let me ruin them myself)
And warns me about thieves and moths and women-
Nothing for money, all for neighborhood."

(Mrs. L, a fussy busybody, spies the root of Ambiguity's tree) "And

      we rode the hairy serpent through the grass
      To the edge of the rectangle she was turning up,
      But he was saying nothing, by his depth
      or diameter, about which way he'd come from."

Poet & Muse   you two pause
                      for coffee.

That's when you, William the Pen
notice the root of all poetry
                        is (quite)
Quotidian:

      "Dishtowels and her nylon underwear
      Were on the clothes tree; straining at the door Was
      her Mercedes. It was half past eight.
      We sat in the kitchen on her good antiques.

Enabling Love   Tom Kirlin

          'Have you ever really thought about the roots.'
          She asked, filling a pair of luster cups,
          'What a world they are, swaying in the thick air
          Under us, upside down?'

Your answer would move Socrates:

                            I'd thought about them
          All the week before, when the elms were budding
          ... And I'd thought how their roots all year
          around Would keep that primavera delicacy.
          So I said, 'I have, a little. What about

them?' That's when She(lley) says:

        '"When I was a girl, my father put those
        cedars In the hedge along the road. He told
        me then... That a tree repeats its structure, up
        and down, The roots mirroring the branches
        ...."

      (A mild disagreement ensues   about trees   in

               Fragonard) and Mrs. L (being Frostian)

claims Shelley's   Figures
               look like...
               Roots.

No, more
     like coral, you, William the Aviator say.

               Mrs. Leamington (immediately) proceeds
to pull out
her:

               "book of reproductions
And showed me the lady swinging on the
swing In a mass of greenery and silk and
cloud.

Then suddenly she turned it upside down
And the cloudy leaves and the clouds turned into rocks

Tom Kirlin   *It Was May*

        And the boles of the tree were gripping them like rocks."

That's when Mrs. L. concludes
her
        (poetic)   about Shelley, a Poet who

Homily (as you so often do)

        "'...met his own image walking in the garden.
        That apparition, sole of men, he saw.
        For know there are two worlds of life and
        death: One which thou beholdest; but the
        other
        Is underneath the grave, where do inhabit
        The shadows of all forms that think and
        live,
        Till death unite them and they part no more....

        "'The strangest thing would be to meet
        yourself. Above the ground or below I
        wouldn't like it.'"
                                        Roots

Dear William, how far you have traveled
        from

        "War's unfeatured
        face"   (where)

        "The far-off dying are her near
   affair; With her sprung creatures become weak or
     strong
She watches them down the sky and disappear,
     Heart gone, sea-bound, committed all to air."
                            Carrier

    William   Morris   Meredith, Jr.

I do   believe

you first TRULY stepped

                              ashore

Enabling Love　　　　　　　　　　　　　　　　　　Tom Kirlin

　　from

War's scalloped, blood-
stained
　　　　　　　　Seas

walking

　　through
　　　　Shelly's MAZE

　　of
　　Allegory.　　　　　For, as you say:

"Shelley's houses and walks were always a clutter of women,
And god knows what further arrangements he kept in his mind.
Drole de menage, Rimbaud said of himself and Verlaine,
As if there were any other kind.
In Yeats' tower, in all that fakery of ghosts,
Some solid women came and slept as Mrs. Yeats'
guests. We are most our own strange selves when we
are hosts."

　　　　　　　　　　　　　　　Five Accouns Of A
　　　　　　　　　　　　　　　Monagomous Man
　　　　　　　　　　　　　　　v. linesfrom his guest-book

So...　　back　　(for the
　　moment) to Mrs. Lemington.

　　　　　Once scattered as a cloud,
　　　　　your Muse

　grew eager to go:

"'back to my spuds, she said. Don't you hate that
word? Yet it's good Middle English. Stop on your
way home. By then perhaps we'll both have earned
a drink.'"
　　　　　　　　　　　　　　　　Roots

William the Aviator has met his match, his Muse

Tom Kirlin   *It Was May*

              and Knows she

"...likes to split an apple down the middle
And with her hands behind her back ask them,
which? The other children fall in with the
riddle
But he says, both hands! both hands, you sly old bitch!"

                        the poet as troublemaker"

Ah! Such a
    World-
    view

              brings

              with

                it

              A World
(of

troubles).

A world
You   take Root

    (and we)

grow into.

I V
The End of Deception

"There is no end to the
Deception of quiet
things And of quiet,
everyday People a
lifetime brings."

The Chinese Banyan

Tom Kirlin   *The End of Deception*

        The Korean War
           exhumed
         the
                Grief
                        you carried
                              (always...)

  nay
                  Embraced
its Stoic
musings

                as you watched

     Worlds at War
        and
                y/our
    (Grecian)

        Urn
        shatter
        :

"...what is it in suffering dismays us more:
The capriciousness with which it is
dispensed Or the unflinching way we see it
borne?

Ah, now she looks at me. We are unmasked
And exchange what roles we guess at for an instant.
The questions Who comes next and Why not me
Rage at and founder my philosophy.
Guilt beyond my error and grace past her
grief Alter the coins I tender cowardly,
Shiver the porcelain fable to green shards."
                      A Korean Woman Seated
                      By A Wall

Enabling Love   Tom Kirlin

No longer
    content with such sentiments
        as those you told

    yourself in pastoral youth,

    when

        "Days like today we are the clouds' men
            And what they do all day is our concern."
                The Impressment

You grew into

        A Field of   VISION

                w   d   e   n ing

    your reach
        as you began to speak

        Directly
        to
        your
        audience.

Sentences   grow

        COMMUNA

        L

–more than a few
laced with
    (in)temperate
    regret
that even Grief
    can become

a commodity:
> "My desperate friends, I want to
> tell Them, you take too delicate
> offense

At the stench of time and man's own smell.
It is only the smell of consequence."

Consequences: i. of choice

Now, when you speak

    to a (post-
    war)
    Audience   I feel each distance   GROW

        (as, quietly, we fall to y/our

        knees) and loudly praise

    St. Consequence
        as if sanity could take shore-leave

from War's Cathedral:

        "Let saints and painters deal
        With the mystery of likeness. *As* for
        him It scares him wide awake and
        dead alone. A man of action dials
        the telephone."
                Barcelona

As your friend Auden said: "poetry changes
    nothing." [maybe; except those who read &
    write it?]

Such extreme feelings,

    grow (once,

        briefly)

        into a

        Self-Effacing
        Mask

Enabling Love   Tom Kirlin

        (an affliction not uncommon at the
        time of Berryman and Lowell)

which you later name:

        Hazard, the Painter.

But before
      we wander on ahead
          let me
              P
                      E
              E
              K

                              at what

several ART - poems
                say

        about the

                LIMiitations
                                of

                Human Speech,

You start with the Body's Splendor:

"With flanks as clean as bone they signal one another
On the far side of a trench of music-
Such breasts and hair, such bold genitals
Until you would think we were the caged ones....

Yet it is not only their perfection detains
Us in the paunchy dark, it is pity too.
That they must signal that way, like eloquent mutes?

Tom Kirlin   *The End of Deception*

       Yes, and a longer affliction of
       splendor: That it cannot   *The Ballet*
       reproduce its kind."

This submerged admission
    of human-kind's limited

                Linguistic
                AMPLITUD
     hums   E

                beneath

       the surface of your
    own SUBdued
        artistic order, Sir William, which

you later acknowledge:

    "It's not the tunes, although as I get
    older Arias are what I hum and whistle.
    It's not the plots-they continue to bewilder
    In the tongue I speak and in several that I wrestle.

    An image of articulateness is what it is:
    Isn't this how we've always longed to
    talk?

    ...these measured cries [opposite] the clumsy things we
    say In the heart's duresses, on the heart's behalf."
                                    About Opera

      I may make more of what you see and feel or

say than you intend,

        the end of

• *Enabling Love*　　　　　　　　　　　　　　　　　Tom Kirlin

    Self-Deception

a deeperrisks our discovering
 a deeper truth

            -the Death of Empathy-
which
      HOVers

         just ahead

     for
     us

     and (if in
         forgetfulness)
    you.

v
Self-Reckoning

"At the edge of the Greek world, I think, was a
cliff To which fallen gods are chained, immortal.
Time is without forgiveness, but
intermittently He sends the old, sentimental,
hungry
Vulture compassion to gnaw on the
stone Vitals of each of us, even the
young, as if
To ready each of us, even the old, for an unthinkable
Event he foresees for each of us-a reckoning, our
own."

Last Things

Tom Kirlin   *Self-Reckoning*

Hazard the
Painter   is neither
                                   Greek
                                   god

nor
      shattere
      d   (Grecian) Urn.

                              He is the MASK

            you   William the Artist

      don
                   (it seems to me)
                            briefly

                   to

                   S P L   I   T

                                          yourself in two

      to   MOCK

                     the
              world the limits
              of
                  ART   with wit
                                and Irony.

              Life's   PUNch
                        line?

                         The artist is

                     "strickly a one-joke painter."

                              [she/he must tell the truth]

Enabling Love   Tom Kirlin

Or, in Hazard's words, as he examines
Meredith's word-paintings:

"The fact that I don't like his pictures
should not obscure the facts
that he is a good man
that many admire his work (his
canvases threaten my existence and
Ihope
mine his, the intolerant bastard!)
that we are brothers in
humanity
& the art. Often it does, though."
                                        Hazard Faces a Sunday
                                        in the Decline

    Some might say this line of argument

CONFUSE
s   Biography
    mit
   Poetry

       but
       William
       launche
       s

     His self-critique

        by dangling

    UP Side

         D
         O
         w
         N

           inside his

Tom Kirlin   *Self Reckoning*

                Craft
        (literally).

"Harnessed and zipped on a
bright October day, having lied to
his wife, Hazard jumps, and the
silk spanks open, and he is falling
safely.

This is what for two years now
he has been painting, in a child's palette
—not the plotted landscape that holds dim
below him, but the human figure dangling
safe, g11yed to something silky, hanging here,
full of half-remembered instruction
but falling, and safe.

[Safe for now, but, like
              other poets
William carries
     an EXTRAordinary
          burden—what to make and say
          of the 1960s and 70s?]

He is in charge of morale in a morbid time.
He calls out to the sky, his voice
the voice of an animal that makes not
words but a happy incorrigible noise, not
of this time. The colors of autumn
are becoming audible though the haze.

It does not matter that the great
masters could see this without flight,
while
dull Hazard must be taken up again and
dropped. He sees it. Then he sees himself....
Inside the bug-like goggles, his eyes water."
                              Hazard's Optimism

Enabling Love   Tom Kirlin

This Icarus flight
-inward-to artistic
boundaries
          offers young poets
     rare
                  (and

                  courageous)

            glimpses

of the
                IMAGINAtion

      in Limbo

          William
                talking to himself

            (wryly)
EXAMing

     his Life
          and
         Accomplishments

     his "Body of Work":

"I look out these two holes, or I run
into the other two and listen. Is Hazard trapped in here?

I have had on this funny suit for years, it's
getting baggy, but I can still move all the
parts.....

People sometimes touch it, that feels good
although I am deep inside.

I do not find it absurd-is this because
I am used to it? (trapped in it? Where are we? This is
certainly not rubber or a cheap plastic.)

Tom Kirlin   *Self-Reckoning*

If I crawl out of it at night, it comes
snuffling after me and swallows me. It
says

it is looking for pictures. I tell
it it has come to the wrong   *Where He's Staying Now*
man."

So what does the artist

        "in charge of morale in a morbid

time" see and say to himself?

     "Tonight Hazard's father and stepmother are having
     jazz for McGovern. In the old game-room
     the old liberals listen as the quintet builds
     crazy houses out of skin and brass,
     crumbling the house of decorum, everybody
     likes that.

     For decades they have paid for the refurbishing
     of America and they have not got their money's worth.
     Now they listen, hopeful,
     to the hard rock for McGovern."
                                             Politics

Long gone are the Allegories
the colloquies and
        DIALogue
                with Shelly's Muse.

William the Walking Hazard

                          a Revenant
    wandering
    through
              Post-War society

        steps
    past

Enabling Love   Tom Kirlin

                                                   beer cans
          &car accidents

   and into a Lovely, yet Ancient
      (forboding?) Landscape,
          where

                                  "Ladyslippers,
                                  gypsy plants long
                                  absent, have
                                  come
                                  back this cold May.
                                  Erotic, stern
                                  ambiguous
                                  shapes, they can blight
                                  or prosper a
                                  season's footwork
                                  for who finds them."

You, William (now turning back toward
     us) stop   to comtemplate

                                stones & Boulders
                                      (one)
                              as
LARGE
     as
            any Mastodon who

                "came riding here
       like hunters, on their ice-barges,
and where they debarked, they stay.

                  ***

Sometimes [Hazard] digs up sharpened ones,
flints- and quartzes-come-lately, flown here
on the ends of sticks
by hungier men, wrestled to
earth by rabbit or deer, little stones
who rode to their quiet on flesh-barges.

Tom Kirlin   *Self-Reckoning*

                                    ***
What is held in perpetuity? The town
hall with all the records will move off
one day, without legal notice.
The air that's passed through his
lungs or the love through his head
and loins
are more his to keep than this boulder-camp,
ready to move off whenever the hunt
resumes."
                                        Squire Hazzard Walks

              Lessons to be
                    learned
                          from
                                Oblivion??

"He's with Yeats, for adult
education- hand-clapping lessons for
the soul, compulsory singling lessons
for the soul, in his case, tone-deaf.
He agrees with Auden, old people can
show 'what grace of spirit can create,'
modeling the flesh when it's no longer
flashy. That's the kind of lift he wants to
his jowls ....

And there
 is   a way Forward
        (One which Mrs. Leamington would approve):

He is founding a sect for the radical old
freaks you may call them but you're
wrong, who persist in being at home in
the world,
who just naturally feel it's a good bind to be
in, let the young feel as uncanny as they like.
Oldbodies, he calls them affectionately
as he towels his own in the morning
in front of the mirror, not getting any flashier.

He thinks about Titan and Renoir a lot in this connection. Nothing is unseemly that takes it rise in love. If only his energy lasts.

His Plans For Old Age

Enabling Love   Tom Kirlin

        But getting here
   has meant
   expending so much
   (poetic) energy

   Repetition
   has begun to set in:

"Here at the seashore they use the clouds over &
over again, like rented animals in *Aida."*
                                                  Rhode Island

    Quietly, as you lift Hazard's
    Mask

        you, William Meredith,

           give us
                          a

        back (FRACTured)   Poetic VOICE

        in uncanny notes
        that warmly
        recall

  Yeats, at Prayer

        in search of
        Belief:

Tom Kirlin   *Self-Reckoning*

      "Enabling love, roof to this drafty hutch
      ... take care of the haunts who stay with
      us here.

      In a little space for a long while they've walked
      wakeful when we sleep, averting their sad glance
      when we're clumsy with one another, they look
      at something we can't look at yet, they creak the
      boards beside the bed we creak, in some hard
      durance.

      And if we're weary at night what must they
      be? Bed them like us at last under your roof.

                             ***

      [W]ishing our sibling spirits nothing but good,
      let them see these chambers once with the daylight
      eyes you lend to lovers for our mortal time.
      Or change some loveless stalker into me
      before my bone-house clatters into
      lime."
                                The Ghosts of the House

    And your
                    E
                    N
                    ABLIN
                    G
                                          Love
        is spoken to one
        person and to ALL
        the living:

              "What you have given me,
                in these long moments when our
                words come back, or breaths come
              back,
              is a whole man at last,
                and keeping me, remembers:

On deck one night, the moon past
full coming up over the planet's edge,
the big globe ripping its skin,
the smaller already accepting its waning

Enabling Love　　　　　　　　　　　　　　　　　　　Tom Kirlin

and talking about vast skiey
distances. I had not met you yet.
Aft, the aircraft folded like mantises,
ahead and abeam, destroyers running like
hounds, and the wind.

A sentry walked off
the rolled front of the flight
deck, crying *oh* as he fell to the
sea.
Lost in the cold skin of the
globe, he cried *oh* for less than,
panted for less than love, going
away,　　　　　　　　　　　　　　　　*February 14*
the loneliest noise that ever wound in my
ear.

No longer
    at Sea,

      you've firmly
      Planted
      your Feet

in American Literature,

                  your Poems
        have become
            Sentries
                to every
                    attentive
                Generation:

      "Gnawed by a vision of
      rightness that no one else
      seems to see, what can a man
      do
      but bear witness?

Tom Kirlin   *Self Reckoning*

        And what has he got to tell?
        Only the shaped things he's
        seen- a few things made by
        men,
        a galaxy made well.

        Though more of each day is
        dark, though he's awkward at
        the job
        he squeezes paint from the
        tube. Hazard is back at
        work.
                              Winter: He Shapes Up

And
yet….   Bea
r Witness
                to

                        what?

                          And how long, how Large

        grows
                      DARKness????

VI
The Center Cannot Hold

"When I wake up, what am I to do
with this mortifying life I've saved again?"
Freezing. iv

Tom Kirlin *The Center Cannot Hold*

The first hint is more than a hunch:

> "I dreamt once they caught me and, holding me
> down, Burned my genitals with gasoline;
> In my stupid terror I was telling them names
> So my manhood kept and the rest went up in flames.
>
> 'Now, say the world is a fair place,' the biggest one
> said, And because there was no face worse than my
> own there I said it and got up. Quite a lot of me is
> charred.
> By our code it is fair. We play fair. The world is fair."
> *Consequences. iii. my acts*

And still the question hangs there
        as if, like Hazard,

                              upside/down:

> "what am I to do
> with this mortifying life I've saved again?

You answer yourself with a parable:

                v.

To live out our lives under a good tyrant
is a lot to ask, the old man said.
There are reports that the swaggering brothers
and their wives and foreign in-laws
are shouting again, in the marble house
that looks down on the harbor and the town.
We know what they are capable of,
quarreling with one another
and in contention with the gods.
We keep indoors.
Impatience and ignorance sometimes ignite
in a flash of bravery among us,
he said. It is usually inappropriate.

Enabling Love   Tom Kirlin

vi

Some normal excellence, of long accomplish
ment is all that can justify our sly survivals.
Freezing

Your answer, I believe, builds on an earlier dream:

"(Sea-brothers, I lower to you the ingenuity of dreams, Strange
lungs and bells to excape in; let me stay aboard last We amend
our dreams in half-sleep. Then it seems
Easy to talk to the severe dead and explain the
past. Now they are saying, Do not be ashamed to stay
alive, You have dreamt nothing that we do not forgive.
And gentlier, Study something deeper than yourselves,
As, how the heart, when it turns diver, delves and saves.)"
                                    The Wreck of the Thresher

As does the artistic mask that
         first surfaced and

                 "settled like a sly disguise
                     On [the Korean woman's] cheerful old face."

In old age, there is nothing hiding
         to or for or from.

"Like black duennas the hours sit
And read our lips and watch our thighs.
The years are pederasts: they
wait for boys and will not meet
my eyes.

Two shapes it has traced honor this right
hand: The curve that a plane rides out
As it leaves or takes a deck on the scalloped sea...

Tom Kirlin   *The Center Cannot Hold*

> And... his gauche fellow, moving
> symetrically Having described one body so
> well
> They could dress that shape in air...."
> *Five Accounts of the Monogomous Man*

Your Enabled
Love   slips an arm

                around

                    Richard'
                                  waist,
              s

        He who meets your

    Revenant
             in lost shapes

      He who carries

        Your

                  We

               ight

             up
               &   D
                     O
                      w
                       N

          stairs, tending

to the

Legacy.

        All of which is as it should
be, for: "The light
of love gilds but does not alter.
People don't change one another

Enabling Love Tom Kirlin

        The only correction is
        by you of you, by me of me....

                every last creature
        is the one it meant to be."
            Consequences: Of Love

Kind words that open   a door
            to Harsh Reality,

     dear   William the

                Pen, (especially)

  IF? If?? When???

                one

              Applies that

              Wisdom
              to your

Later Poetic
career   which begins
                  with this sentiment:

VII
Efforts at Speech

"Cheer or courage is what [poems] were all
born in. It's what they're trying to tell us,
miming like that. It's native to the words,
and what they want us always to know,
even when it seems quite impossible to do."

The Cheer

Tom Kirlin   *Efforts at Speech*

    Having   Praised,
                       Honored, nay,
                       Believed

Shelley Auden Frost Yeats

        (so lawyerly the

      way EACH
      adjudicates
   fear/   speech)

you now measure
      yourself (harshly)
  against

        COnTEmporarie
      s   (generously,

       repeating
       each given
       name
     a telling feat)

       Richard Wilbur
  Wallace Stevens
      Robert Lowell
      (again) Ernest
      Hemingway Sylvia
      Plath
      John Berryman (again and
      again) Kurt Vonnegut
  Until a   Sigmund Freud

      STROKE
              tore You r

Enabling Love   Tom Kirlin

```
            T
             O      from   B
            N        R      from  L
           G          A
            u                              M
            E          N             B....
```

"Expressive Aphasia"

                                                doctors
call it.

              But   it seems

(to me)
                  you   already

     KNEW   and   had NAMED
                        it:

  "Effort at Speech."

                  And   (again)

It's a

         brown-faced

      boy
             of fifteen or sixteen
                  (his face
                  "phrased like a
                  question")

            who ROBS
                you of the Pen:

"Half of the papers lending me a name are
                   gone with him nameless"

Tom Kirlin   *Efforts at Speech*

      Your Wreck   (still)

        produc

        es   Hope Suffering

        Anguis   among dear Friends

        h

    but most
    (in retrospect)

              I suspect

Calm

      in those who never

Claimed
      your embrace
                   or shared
     your keen
     ATTention.

    So, later, after

        Adult On-set Autism,

                      to

    watch   you
              swim
              the
              Ocean of

        COURAGE
             makes us all want to

C
 R
   A
    W
     L

Enabling Love   Tom Kirlin

    through tears.

        Even as You

            Lamented

                SUicide

      among writers, Poets,

    Friends

(and yet)
    REFUSed
               to
                sin
                k

                        into
                        Depressio
                        n

        or   self-pity.

Instead, on first meeting
you I Imagined
        Your
                Imagination

  (looking out those holes)

  Not as Hazard, behind a mask

        but an an ARTist robbed of

            Expressive
            Anticipation,
            who kept:

Tom Kirlin   *Efforts at Speech* ·

"Walking home [as] I fraternized
with shadows, Zig-zagging with them where they flee the
streetlights,
Asking for trouble, asking for the message
                          trouble had sent me.

Allfall down has been scribbled on the
street in Garbage and excrement: so
much for the vision Others taunt me
with, my untimely humor,
                    so much for cheerfulness.

Next time don't wrangle, give the boy the money,
Call across chasms what the world you know is.
Luckless and lied to, how can a child master
                              human decorum?

Next time a switch-blade, somewhere he is thinking,
I should have killed him and took the lousy wallet.
Reading my cards he feels a surge of anger
                          blind as my shame.

Error from Babel mutters in the places,
Cities apart, where now we word our failures:
Hatred and guilt have left us without language
                    who might have held discourse.
                              Effort at Speech

           No longer submerged
Grief
               stakes
       its
                  (starke
                  r)
                  claim
                  to
                  Days of Silent Sanity:

Enabling Love   Tom Kirlin

"Whether we give assent to this or rage
Is a question of temperament and does not
matter. Some will has been done past our
understanding, Past our guilt surely equal to
our fears.
Dullards, we are set again to the cryptic blank
page Where the sea schools us with terrible
water.
The noise of a boat breaking up and its men is in our
ears. The bottom here is too far down for our
sounding.
The ocean was salt before we crawled to tears.
                                               The Wreck of the Thresher

Silence
         alon
        e   answers that "sly old
                                                             bitch" of youth

                      who hides Poetic Truth
                                                  (from all of us)
                and holds out
                       Both
                       Hands like:

"The woman who sailed her dinghy out in the
Bay in the fall blow-autumn is for
beginnings-
and was found miles from the zig-zagging
sailboat that she knew like a husband either
she sought
a way to drown or the Chesapeake taught her, not both.

Either before I die I'll falter and tell
the strange secret I was given once as a
token or I'll manage to carry it with me.

Somebody knows or nobody knows these answers.

One of those appalling things is true too."

Not Both

        Equally true

William, is your Strength
    of Spirit

which shines
        through

        a second "Crossing Over"

           (into)

poetic SPEECH:

    "That's what love is like. The whole river
    is melting. We skim along in great peril,

    having to move faster than ice goes under
    and still find foothold in the soft floe."
                            Crossing Over

And, though said to one, you shared with us all in poetry:

    "How perilous in one another's V
    our lives are, yoked in this yoke:
    two men, leaning apart for light,
    but in a wind who give each other lee."
                      A Couple of Trees

VI
Impartial Laugher

"It is like finding on your tongue right words to call across the floe of arrogance to the wise dead,
of health to sickness, old to young Across this debt, we tell you so."

Talking Back
[To W.H. Auden}

Tom Kirlin   *Impartial Laughter*

                  What
                        (more)
                                do
                  we LNing
                              owe

                    you

                    wh
                    o
                    M
                            O
                            v
                                  e
(among)   us

            like a chill breeze

                            Scattering

Memorials, Birthdays,   holidays, Poems, Trips,

          Lovers, Articles, Books

Prizes
                    &&
                                such

                    Generosit
                  y

that   ARTeries of
              Friendshi
              p

    harden into trees

        that a

Racoon would love to

climb
        even for the   Briefest

    chance to meet???

Enabling Love   Tom Kirlin

        Beyond reading
        your Essays, Reviews
        Meeing   the Acolytes   Students

        Revisting Conversations
                Praising the Grants, Awards

        (twice, you were honored by the Library of

                Congress) We take
                Pleasure

          in your Feast
          of   Poems

                gristled
                      with   Hard Truths.

And, Yes,   of course,

            we still will visit
            you in

            (new)

      LONDON
                Connectic
                ut   (your ashes also
   in
                  Bulgarias
   Rila
   Monestary).

            But mostly
                (and most personally)

                      I will continue to
  REcall

that first meeting

at your party, in Bethesda, Maryland.

I had not yet greeted you
properly
       (even on a poetic
       trip)
but in that private session
you asked me to recite a poem
and once I did, you gripped affliction
by the throat and troubled out
fair words and lasting impressions.

Afterwards, happy to be included
you moved among we chatty few
picking up lipsticked glasses
from coffee tables, placing some
on countertops

as through it all, smiled and nodded encouragement
at this or that thought, a turn of phrase, caught
expressions. You clearly lived, in silence
the spellbound muse, then of a tender age
somewhat of scattered tongue
full of goodwill, grace and emotions unsung.

I suppose we relish most what most we choose
but like that witch who demanded
in youth one hand, you answered "both"
and now, in age, your smile
wryly countered: "neither."

We poets often break one simple rule,
 the truce between silence, death and
truth —and so sing out childish unfit
rhymes until in time life masters us
and we become finger-food.

Meantime, patterned as china, you gathered us
up that day, filling the room with senseless music.
Your crooked smile outlasts
the body, your poems now our muse.

VI
Epilogue

Why the Soul Loves Catfish
To William Meredith

Let's just say an elegant man
in a loose blue nightcap
with nothing, nothing on his mind
but the sky, surprised us
tracking game by starlight

shot you in the blind
made off with the lamps
of madness & climbed
scattering as ransom
this palpable absence

only time can refine—
swirling her honey head
making our bed, as constant
as taxes & crime....So welcome
if you can, ladies & gentlemen

an old roommate of mine:
a son of a gun—a hell
of a guy—a cat whose ass
rattles buckshot—the warden
my soul, serving life, plus 99.

Examples of Created Systems
    For Robert Penn Warren and Eleanor Clark

i. the stars

We look out at them on clear nights, thrilled
rather than comforted—brilliance and
distance put us in mind of our

own burnings and losses. And then who
flung them there, in a sowing motion
suggesting that random is beautiful?

ii. archipelagoes

Or again, the islands that the old
cartographers, triangulating
their first glimpses of bays and peaks, set
down, and which the rich traveler, from
a high winter chair, chooses among
today—chains of jade thrown across the
torso of the sea-mother, herself
casually composed.

Enabling Love 　　　　　　　　　　　　　　　Tom Kirlin

iii. work camps and

prisons The homeless
Solzhenitsyn, looking at
Russia, saw a configuration of
camps
spotting his homeland, 'ports' where
men and women were forced to act
out
the birth-throes of volcanic
islands, the coral patience of reefs,
before
a 'ship,' a prison train, bore them
down that terrible archipelago
conceived and made by men like ourselves.

iv. those we love

Incorrigibly (it is our nature)
when we look at a map we look
for the towns and valleys and
waterways
where loved people constellate, some of
them from our blood, some from our own loins.
This fair scattering of matter
is all we will know of creation,
at
first hand. We flung it there, in a
learned gesture of sowing-random,
lovely.

　　　　　　　　　　　　　　-William Meredith

Tom and Katherine Kirlin at New Year's celebratinon at the Bethesda hosue

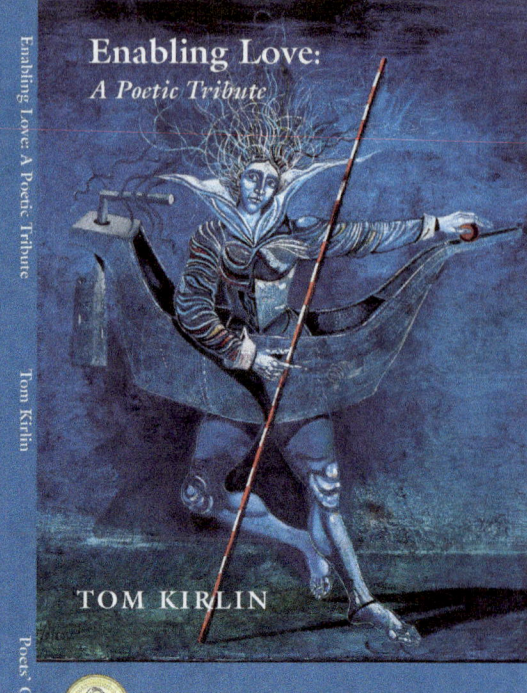

Enabling Love:
A Poetic Tribute

TOM KIRLIN

Winner of the 2019
William Meredith Award in Poetry

ENABLING LOVE traces Tom Kirlin's long journey toward a deep understanding and empathy for the poetry of William Meredith. It is an appreciation based on years of friendship between the two poets in a format that is as complex as the mind of Meredith himself. Like an exquisite jigsaw puzzle or crossword, Kirlin plays with language through puns, synecdoche, broken word fragments, and provocative enjambments to give heightened meaning to Meredith's poetry. The style is challenging, but worth the effort as we follow Kirlin's exploration and the loving attention he gives to his colleague in the art. It is a fitting centenary tribute to a poet who has been described as a national treasure and lucky inheritance. We are equally lucky to have Kirlin's intense magnifying glass, enabling love.

Tom Kirlin won the Larry Neal Award for Poetry. He also received a grant from the District of Columbia Commission on the Arts and a fellowship from the National Endowment for the Humanities for post-doctoral studies at Yale University. He taught at the University of Wisconsin-Madison before moving to Washington, DC, where he worked for several decades on energy, environment, science and technology policy issues, including the UN climate negotiations and the Kyoto Protocols. He later served as Vice President of the Center for the Study of the Presidency, a non-partisan group he helped rebuild. Following a summer at Bread Loaf, his first book of poems, *Under the Potato Moon*, was published by the Little Red Tree Press in 2013. Other poems have appeared in *Hungry as We Are*, *The WPFW Poetry Anthology*, and *Cabin Fever*. He and his wife, Katherine, helped celebrate the Smithsonian Institution's 25th Folklife Festival by collecting recipes and authoring the *Smithsonian Folklife Cookbook*.

William Meredith's was an extraordinary life. Poet, arborist and beloved teacher at Connecticut College for nearly 40 years, poetry, trees and students were his major preoccupations in life. He served as a Navy pilot in WWII and Korea ("I'd respect you for that if for nothing else," Robert Frost told him once when William described the thirty-two night landings he made on an aircraft carrier during the war.) Meredith was awarded the Pulitzer Prize, the National Book Award and the LA Times Book Award, all of which came after the challenges of a major stroke, and his work has received many additional American and international awards. In 1996, he was accorded Bulgarian citizenship by President Zhelu Zhelev for the bridge he created between our two countries. "If Poetry were landscape, Meredith would be a National Park," William Matthews once said of Meredith's poetry.

Stoimen Stoilov

1944 Born in Varna (Bulgaria)
1972 Graduated from the Academy of Fine Arts in Sofia (Bulgaria).
Lives and works in Vienna (Austria) since 1991.

ONE-PERSON EXHIBITIONS IN:

Australia, Austria, Bulgaria, Canada, Czech Republic, France, Finland, Germany, Italy, Japan, Luxembourg, Norway, Russian Federation, Slovakia, Sweden, Switzerland, United States of America.

BIENNALES AND SALONS

Print Biennale, Varna (Bulgaria); Europ Art, Geneva (Switzerland); International Print Triennale, Chamallières (France); Biennale des artistes jurassiens, Delemont (Switzerland); Print Biennale, Ljubljana (Slovenia); Salon d'automne, Paris (France); Print Biennale, Fredrikstad (Norway); Print Biennale, Cracow (Poland); International Print Exhibition, Biella (Italy); Art Expo, New York (USA); Salon du dessin et de la peinture à l'eau, Paris (France); Print Biennale, Sao Paulo (Brazil); Biennale, Brno (Czech Republic); Biennale, Bratislava (Slovakia)

PRIZES

2009 The title Professor
1991 Gottfried von Herder Prize for his complete works, University of Vienna (Austria)
1991 Prize at the 2nd Print Triennale, Chamallières (France)

1985 Grand Prix for Bulgarian Participants at the 3rd Print Biennale, Varna (Bulgaria)
1984 Prize at Art Expo, New York (USA), granted by the foundation Bilan de l'art contemporain.
1983 The 'Iliya Petrov' Grand Prix for Mural Painting awarded by the Union of Bulgarian Artists, Sofia (Bulgaria)
1982 Silver Medal at the International Exhibition in Leipzig (Germany)
1976 Grand Prix of the Biennale, Brno (Czech Republic)

He has been awarded many other national prizes for print and drawing.

PRIVATE COLLECTIONS AND MUSEUMS

Austria
Museum of Graphic Art Albertina, Vienna
Vienna Ministry of Foreign Affairs, Vienna
Artothek, Vienna

Bulgaria
The National Art Gallery, Sofia
Municipal Museum of Art, Varna

France
Bibliothque nationale de France, Paris
Fonds national d'art contemporain, Paris
Art Dialogue Foundation, Paris

Germany
Museum of Art Villa Merkel, Esslingen
Museum of Graphic Art of the Schreiner Foundation, Bad Steben
Ludwig Forum, Aachen

Russia
Pushkin Museum of Art, Moscow

USA.
The Library of Congress, Washington DC
New York Public Library
Princeton University
Yale University
Florida State University (Strozier Library)
Florida Atlantic University (Jaffe Collection)
Middlebury College (Starr Library)

Works in private collections:
Austria, Australia, Bulgaria, France, Finland, Germany, Japan, Luxembourg, Norway, Sweden, and the United States of America.

MEREDITH POEMS FROM EFFORT AT SPEECH

Love Letter from an Impossible Land

June: Dutch Harbor   To Charles Shain

In June, which is still June here, but once removed

From other Junes, chill beardless high-voiced cousin season,

The turf slides grow to an emerald green.

There between the white-and-black of the snow and ash,

Between the weak blue of the rare sky

Or the milkwhite languid gestures of the fog,

And the all-the-time wicked terminal sea,

There, there, like patches of green neon,

See it is June with the turf slides.

Where the snow streams crease the fields darkly

The rite of flowers is observed, and because it is a new land

There is no great regard to precedent:

Violets the size of pansies, the huge anemone,

Sea-wishing lupine that totters to the brink;

Others are: wild geranium, flag, cranberry, a kind of buttercup.

In the morning sandpipers stumble on the steel mats,

Sparrows sing on the gun, faraway eagles are like eagles.

On the map it says, The Entire Aleutian Chain Is a Bird Sanctuary,

And below, Military Reservation: This Airspace To Be Flown Over Only

by Authority of the Secretary of the Navy.

Fly just above the always-griping sea

That bitches at the bitter rock the mountains throw to it,

Fly there with the permission—subject always to revoke—

Of the proper authorities,

Under milkwhite weagving limbs of the fog,

Past the hurriedly erected monuments to you,

Past the black and past the very green

But for your car, jeweled and apopinted all for no delight,

But for the strips that scar the islands that you need,

But for your business, you could makd a myth.

Though you are drawn by a thousand remarkable horses

On fat silver wings with a factor of safety of four,

And are sutured with steel below and behind and before,

And can know with your fingers the slightest unbalance of forces,

Your mission is smaller than Siegfried's, lighter than Tristan's,

And there is about it a certain undignified haste.

Even with flaps there is a safe minimum;

Below that the bottom is likely to drop out.

Some of the soldiers pressed flowers in June, indicating faith;

The one who knew all about birds spun in that month.

It is hard to keep your mind on war, with all that green

New Poems (1958–83) from Effort At Speech

  His Students
In the warm classroom, they give off heat.
It is winter, the lights are on, the pipes knock.
We are studying their youth. I talk.
I don't have a doctorate, but I know
The old way things were done and why.
Formerly I too was young. I sweat.
I've always believed in manners, and to this day
I will defend them. They are a small part of the truth.

I have become fond of this class. Dressed and coiffed
and intellectually equipped like so many Kaspar Hausers,*
they struggle into the Nürnberg of my Tuesdays,
taxing my powers of invention. Now they are asking
personal questions which do not bear
on youth, which have nothing to do with the subject,
youth. There's an atmosphere of guarded trust
in the room and I don't want to appear pedantic,
but after all, I am the instructor,
they sought me out. Or did I seek them out?

As they ask nosy, characteristic questions
I realize how interested I am in them
as young men and women, in their personal lives.
You can't study youth apart from the world
it has made, personally, out of the damnedest junk.
Nor are they as guileless as they pretend,
all raising their hands at once when I ask
who would like to explain age? Whoever I call on
will say something that sounds like his last respects.

I study them hard, but they will barely consent to leaf
through me, or their stereotype for me.
I wonder if I will ever be read again
after the present generation of teachers retires?
So I read excerpts to them. I read a passage about an old war.
It is curiously lacking in violence (I shy
away from holocaust, just as they are obsessed with it),
but what I read is true and they are impressed.
How much better it sounds when I read it!
Perhaps it isn't really there on the page?
merely a trick of reading, a gift for explanation?

Meantime before the bell I remember to summarize.
(They won't do these things for themselves—
their notebooks are graffiti, though I still
ask that they be passed in at intervals.)
I summarize as impartially as I know how,
the essential differences, touched on this hour,
between youth and its opposite, age.

*Kaspar Hauser: 1812?–33, mysterious German foundling. He appeared in Nuremberg in 1828 in a state of semi-idiocy, and giving an incoherent account of his past, which he said he had spent in a dark prison hole.

Journal Entry (With the Udalls, June 1968)

The moon came up late, because the sandstone bluff across the river rises perhaps 50 degrees from where I'd set my sleeping bag. First the cliff behind me took moonlight, then I sat up to watch the canyon wall running NE above us take color. The reds emerged in the light of the full moon, the way I have occasionally seen autumn sumac and maple tell color by moonlight, or I suppose roses must do: I can't recall roses by moonlight though I must have seen them.

Finally toward the top of the bluff the glow became brighter and at last, only 30 or 40 feet below the top, the moon put out a bright edge, making the dark edge of the bluff dance on the retina. How many million times has this night of the planet's tilt occurred before there was a viewer from this crevice in the sand?

Later I woke and walked across the brilliant sand, past sleepers, to the edge of the bright rapids. Once there was a meteorite in the western notch where the Dipper was going away, lip-first. Then the moon was eaten by the opposite bluff, the one we slept under, having described a low southern arc, like the winter sun's. In the full moon, on my sleeping bag, I had been able to see to write with this pen a little tetrameter sonnet.

  In the Canyon

Under the massive cliffs which the moon,
miser of color, gives color to,
on moon-colored sand at the end of June
hearing the rapids we've hurtled through,
seeing at the base of the talus strand
off the further shore, the whitewater crest
in the frenzy of running water stands,
and Scorpio follows the Dipper west.

The troubles of cities do not recede
from the mind. Rather, they nag like guilt,
as sometimes when I drink and feed,
in my delicate gluttony I've felt
the spectral hunger of Asia bite
my gut and whet my appetite.

English Accounts

I. Trelawny's Dream

Edward John Trelawny, who is imagined to speak the following lines in his late middle age, survived his friend Shelley by almost sixty years, and lies beside him in the Protestant Cemetery in Rome. He seems to have met no man or woman in a long life whom he could marvel at and love as he did Shelley. Trelawny had intended to convoy the poet and Edward Williams (and a cabin boy, Charles Vivian) when they sailed the Ariel out of Leghorn into the storm that drowned them, but Lord Byron's yacht, which he was commanding, was detained at the last minute by port authorities. He cremated the remains of his friends, and recovered the little boat, which appeared to have been run down by a larger vessel, though the violent squall into which the Ariel disappeared would have been enough to founder the keel-heavy boat which Trelawny himself had unwisely designed for the novice Shelley.
—W. M.

The dark illumination of a storm
and water-noise, chuckling along the hull
as the craft runs tight before it.
Sometimes Shelley's laughter wakes me here,
unafraid, as he was the day he dove
into water for the first time, a wooded pool
on the Arno, and lay like a conger eel
on the bottom—'where truth lies,' he said—
until I hauled him up.

But oftener the dream insists on all,
insists on retelling all.
Ned Williams is the first
to see the peril of the squall. His shout
to lower sail scares the deck boy wide-eyed
and cuts off Shelley's watery merriment.
The big wind strokes the catboat like a kitten.
Riding the slate-gray hillocks, she is dragged
by the jib Ned Williams leaves to keep her head.
The kitten knows the wind is a madman's hand
and the bay a madman's lap.
As she scuds helpless, only the cockney boy
Charles Vivian and I, a dreamer and a child,
see the felucca loom abeam. Her wet lateen
ballooning in the squall, she cuts across
wind and seas in a wild tack, she is on us.
The beaked prow wrenches the little cabin
from the deck, tosses the poet slowly to the air—
he pockets his book, he waves to me and smiles __

then to his opposite element,
light going into darkness, gold into lead.
The felucca veers and passes, a glimpse of a face
sly with horror on her deck. I watch our brave
sailor boy stifle his cry of knowledge
as the boat takes fatal water, then Ned's stricken face,
scanning the basalt waves
for what will never be seen again except in dreams.

All this was a long time ago, I remember.
None of them was drowned except me
whom a commotion of years washes over.
They hail me from the dream, they call an old man
to come aboard, these youths on an azure bay.
The waters may keep the dead, as the earth may,
and fire and air. But dream is my element.
Though I am still a strong swimmer
I can feel this channel widen as I swim.

II. Trelawny at Sompting, 1879

Sometimes I dream about those two cauldrons—
the one at Port Louis wherein I placed
the ruby-spangled Arab with my heart.
After the oil and camphor and ambergris,
the dark smoke rose and I sprang forward,
falling on the sand so near the fire
my hands were burned; and the one I had forged
at Leghorn, the iron machine for Ned and Shelley.
Shelley's brain seethed and bubbled but the heart
would not burn—a bright flame stroked and stroked it,
occasioned by a liquid still flowing from it,
and I took it in my hand to examine it,
after shrinking it in sea water, yet
it was still so hot as to burn my hand badly.
The day before, Ned Williams' handkerchief,
whole silk beside his exhumed carrion,
made Byron say, 'The entrails of a worm
hold together longer than the potters' clay
of which man is made.' During the burning,
he swam far out to sea.
If I told Miss Taylor now
to leave the tea things and go gather faggots
and set them under my tub, I could rejoin them,
Zela, Arabian bird, and restless Shelley.

III. In the Protestant Cemetery

How did their lives go out from those deaths,
Keats' at the foot of the Spanish Steps, Shelley's
in the wild wave, accepted on the beach at Leghorn,
frail heroes, riding for sixty years the dreams
of Severn and Trelawny. How did their lives survive?

Who does not envy the young dead? Every year
the odds increase against accomplishment.
There is a thinning out, a dilution. The old
are in desperate trouble. These did not lose their models .

The great old man Severn was painting in Rome when
Trelawny in Sussex wrote to Clare, 'I have
an icy cold bath every morning and then go out
with my shirtsleeves tucked up and work in the garden.'
When they left that century it grew old.

Middle-aged people raised a subscription
to lay the old painter next to his young friend.
The adventurer followed, having lately written
a letter to Rome: 'In the year 1822 I purchased
a piece of land from the then Custodian—
I believe your father—under the pyramid
of Caius Cestius. I deposited the ashes
of my Friend Shelley in the one tomb
and the other I left for my ashes...
We are parodies of boys and girls and we're aging.
After thirty who can think of himself except
as foully wronged, only the satiric overtones vary.
Judging ourselves harshly for natural losses,
we throw ourselves with less and less confidence
on the charity of our youth. We need good examples,
we need these two old men here under the cypresses.

Crossing Over

> It was now early spring, and the river was swollen and turbulent; great cakes of floating ice were swinging heavily to and fro in the turbid waters. Owing to a peculiar form of the shore, on the Kentucky side, the land bending far out into the water, the ice had been lodged and detained in great quantities, and the narrow channel which swept round the bend was full of ice, piled one cake over another, thus forming a temporary barrier to the descending ice, which lodged, and formed a great undulating raft. . . . Eliza stood, for a moment, contemplating this unfavorable aspect of things.
> —Harriet Beecher Stowe, Uncle Tom's Cabin (Chapter VII, "The Mother's Struggle")

That's what love is like. The whole river
is melting. We skim along in great peril,

having to move faster than ice goes under
and still find foothold in the soft floe.

We are one another's floe. Each displaces the weight
of his own need. I am fat as a bloodhound,

hold me up. I won't hurt you. Though I bay,
I would swim with you on my back until the cold

  seeped into my heart. We are committed, we
  we are going across this river willy-nilly.

  No one, black or white, is free in Kentucky,
  old gravity owns everybody. We're weighty.

  I contemplate this unfavorable aspect of things.
  Where is something solid? Only you and me.

  Has anyone ever been to Ohio?
  Do the people there stand firmly on icebergs?

  Here all we have is love, a great undulating
  raft, melting steadily. We go out on it

  anyhow. I love you, I love this fool's walk.
  The thing we have to learn is how to walk light.

Country Stars

The nearsighted child has taken off her glasses
and come downstairs to be kissed goodnight.
She blows on a black windowpane until it's white.
Over the apple trees a great bear passes
but she puts her own construction on the night.

Two cities, a chemical plant, and clotted cars
breathe our distrust of darkness on the air,
clouding the pane between us and the stars.
But have no fear, or only proper fear:
the bright watchers are still there.

Parents

For Vanessa Meredith and Samuel Wolf Gezari

What it must be like to be an angel
or a squirrel, we can imagine sooner.

The last time we go to bed good,
they are there, lying about darkness.

They dandle us once too often,
these friends who become our enemies.

Suddenly one day, their juniors
are as old as we yearn to be.

They get wrinkles where it is better
smooth, odd coughs, and smells.

It is grotesque how they go on
loving us, we go on loving them.

The effrontery, barely imaginable,
of having caused us. And of how.

Their lives: surely
we can do better than that.

This goes on for a long time. Everything
they do is wrong, and the worst thing,

they all do it, is to die,
taking with them the last explanation,

how we came out of the wet sea
or wherever they got us from,
taking the last link
of that chain with them.

Father, mother, we cry, wrinkling,
to our uncomprehending children and grandchildren.

taking the last link
of that chain with them.

Father, mother, we cry, wrinkling,
to our uncomprehending children and grandchildren.

For Two Lovers in the Year 2075 in the
Canadian Woods

If you have lips and forests,
you creatures years from now,
here are some lines to tell you
that we were among your trees
in extraordinary flesh
and ecstasy now gone,
and our tongues looked for each other
and after that for words.
If you have August moonrise
and bodies to undress,
here are some words we've left you
when we had had our say.
Put them beside your cummings,
if you still carry books,
not as sweet as Landor,
not as quick as Donne,
wrap them in still-warm clothing
beside your sleeping bag
for when you want to speak.

These trees are stirred by ghosting,
not only ours but others'.
Enjoy the feathery presences,
no sadder than your own,
they gather from the past—
last August's moan and whisper,
the leaves renew the weavings
and lacings of the flesh.
Here is the sound of ours.

ETCHINGS BY STOIMEN STOILOV TO ILLUSTRATE ECHOES

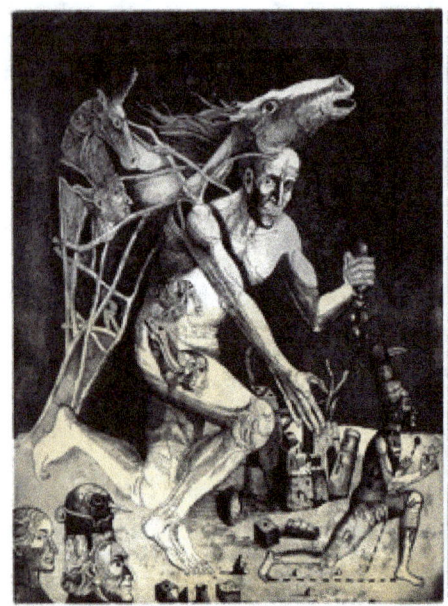

The Hundredth Anniversary of William Meredith,

by Krassin Himmirski,

(Translation through CHROME. Appeared first at the following link:

https://e-lit.info/index.php/lit-teory/1720-2019-02-10-05-51-42)

For the spiritual heritage of the great American poet William Meredith argue two centuries - the XX century and the first decade of the 21st century. His poetry and ideals prove their vitality in our day.

Born in New York on January 9, 1919, in a progressive family. One of his ancestors was Minister of Finance and Republican at the time of Abraham Lincoln and his portrait was printed on American banknotes. In the turbulent post-war years and the depressed depression, his father shares the ideas of socialism.

W. Meredith follows English language and literature in one of the oldest and most prestigious universities in the United States, Princeton University, New Jersey. His diploma work is on the work of American poetry classic Robert Frost.

In the past, Princeton University has completed two American presidents - James Madison and Wodrow Wilson. After his emigration to the United States in the midst of rising fascism in Europe, Albert Einstein worked at the University of Nuclear Energy Institute until the end of his life. Here follows the most prominent representative of the "lost generation" after World War I, the fiction writer Scott Fitzgerald.

After graduating, W. Meredith initially worked as a distributor of the New York Times newspaper, where he was subsequently a reporter and conductor for theater, opera and literature.

William Meredith as a pilot from the US Navy on the Pacific Front during the Second World War.

After the United States entered the Second World War, the young Meredith enrolled a volunteer in the army. He was sent as a pilot at a US aircraft carrier in the Pacific region of the Aleutian Islands. After graduating, W. Meredith initially worked as a distributor of the New York Times newspaper, where he was subsequently a reporter and conductor for theater, opera and literature.

Meeting of William Meredith, US Poet Laureate and Poetry Consultant at the Congress Library in Washington with the Cultural Attaché of the Bulgarian Embassy Krasin Himirski

From the student years he wrote poetry and from the front he sent a large cycle of poems to participate in the Yale University Young Poets Competition. The director of the Library of Congress, prominent poet Archibald McLeish is very impressed with the poetry of the talented combat pilot, featuring gunpowder from the fighting and the decisive battle against Japanese militarism and fascism. He writes an enthusiastic preface to William Meredith's First Poem Book "Letters from an Impossible Land," which came out in 1944.

After the war, he was engaged in lecturing, except in the years of the Korean War. Since 1946, he has been a resident at Princeton University. He has an impressive work experience at a number of universities: the Ringtones, the Hawaiian, Carnegie-Mellon, the American University in Blagoevgrad, the Middlebury College, the Summer Creative Workshops in Bred Loaf. He spent three decades reading lectures at the Connecticut College in New London where he also had his own home. Honorary Doctor is at Carnegie-Mellon University, Princeton University, the American University in Blagoevgrad, Connecticut College.

From 1976 to 1980, he was a poet-laureate of the United States, a poetry consultant at the Library of Congress. He was secretary of the National Academy of Art and Literature and Chancellor of the Academy of American Poets in New York.
He is the winner of the Carl Sandberg Award (1979), the Los Angeles Times Award (1987), the Pulitzer Prize for his poetic book "The Likely Balance" (1988), the Guggenheim Foundation Prize ; He was awarded the Harriet Monroe Medal and the Special Prize and Medal for his overall literary work from

The Culture and Tourism Commission of Connecticut (2007).
He publishes the books: "Ships and Other Figures", "Treshare Cruise", "Winter Poems", "Earth Walk", "Hezard, the Artist", "Optimistic Mood", "Speech Strongness".

Meredith translated from French and published the verses of Guillaume Apollinaire. As editor, he published the anthology "The Little Irish Poets". In 1976 I went to a mandate as a Cultural Attaché of the Bulgarian Embassy in Washington. The Library of Congress, one of the richest libraries in the world, was the second "job" for me after my daily duties and my weekends. The tradition of the library is to present world literatures and authors. In the same year, William Meredith took up the position of the Poet, a laureate of the United States, a poetry consultant at the Library of Congress. I attended all the dinners organized in the library and it was natural to meet the manager.

He introduced me to the library's leadership, and introduced me to a number of his predecessors in this post. Between us, a sincere, perennial friendship has begun, which has continued for the rest of his life. We met regularly both in the library and at home, we traveled to very interesting meetings with famous American writers and cultural figures.

I personally offered W.Meredith to participate in the US committee headed by Senator Fulbright (from a hundred prominent figures of American culture and the arts) to celebrate the 1300th anniversary of the Bulgarian state in the United States. The celebration took place at the highest level in the Dumbarton Oaks Museum building, where the United Nations was founded.

His love for Bulgaria began after he became acquainted with the work of Nikola Vaptsarov. In 1979, the WBS invited William Meredith to take part in celebrating the 70th anniversary of our poet- revolutionary. In his speech at the celebration he made a bold analogy between two great artists of Bulgaria and America. "Your Vaptsarov and our Walt Whitman are intimate lyrical singers. But their songs are not just for comfort. They require us constant vigilance and assertion of freedom. "And it is even more emphasized by speaking of the latest history of our countries: "During the Second World War, many Americans were killed by the same tyranny against which he fought the verses and give your life to Vaptsarov. " Meredith translates verses of Nikola Vaptsarov, which includes in his edited and published anthology "Bulgarian Poets" including the creativity of our 24 creators. In addition, translators are John Updike, Maxin Kumin and Richard Wilbur. Publishing House "Orpheus" publishes the collections with poems by Meredith "The Shadow Observers" and "Partial Descriptions". Elka Nyagolova has translated Meredith's poems in the outspoken book "The White Island".

At the invitation of the Congress Library with the support of Meredith in 1980, a representative group of Bulgarian poets was present in the USA: Georgi Dzagarov, Lyubomir Levchev, Vladimir Golev, Bozhidar Bozhilov and Lachezar Elenkov with translator Vladimir Filipov. Our creators were accepted by the head of the House of Representatives at the US Congress. He also met with the cultural community of the American capital at the home of the poet and translator Elisaveta Richie.

In addition to the Library of Congress, a recital was also held at Pittsburgh at the University of Pennsylvania. In New York, the delegation was accepted by the leadership of the Academy of American Poets and visited the United Nations

The active contacts with the Library of Congress continued in the following years with visits and recitals to Bulgarian artists. Blaga Dimitrova made an independent recital. Interviews with Bulgarian writers Yordan Radichkov, Bozhidar Bozhilov, Nadya Kehlibareva, Zdravko Popov, Petko Bratanov, Nino Nikolov were interviewed and included in the newly created fund for the life of world artists.

In this fund, I also recorded myself by performing my own poems and interview before leaving for Bulgaria at the end of my term. Upon return, I released the poetry book "Washington recitation" with the disc - record in the Library of Congress.
/ 5-1 The Poetry Book "Washington Recite" /

For merit in popularizing Bulgarian literature and developing cultural ties with the United States, William Meredith and Richard Harteis received honorary Bulgarian citizenship under President J. Zhelev's Decree.

After returning from Bulgaria, William Meredith invited me to his annual lecture at Connecticut College. An exhibition of graphics presented to him by Stoimen Stoilov, translations of his poems in Bulgarian and the winning medal of the International Vaptsar Prize was opened in the salons of the college. The same medal Meredith wore as a medal later on.

Since then, William Meredith and his companion, poet Richard Hartness, came to Bulgaria every year. They participated in several of the Sofia International Writing Meetings and in the celebrations for the 1300th Anniversary of the Bulgarian State.

in 1983, Meredith suffered a severe stroke and lost his speech. After spending a year with us together with R. Harteis, rehabilitation and meeting with Baba Vanga, he partially recovered his speech and began to recite his poems again.

We traveled all over Bulgaria: Sandanski, Melnik, Blagoevgrad, Rila Monastery, Vratsa, Bourgas, Varna,
Kavarna, Albena and others.

Our many meetings are unforgettable in my home on 11 Graf Ignatiev Street in Sofia, my home in the villages of Varbitsa, Vratsa and organized joint recitals and presentations throughout the country.

W. Meredith , R. Harteis , I and Stalin Himirski in my home, Varbitsa.

Bulgaria-American Foundation for the Development of Arts was established in Bulgaria with President
William Meredith and Executive Director of My Honor.

There was an idea to build a foundation complex. We held talks with the then Mayor of Kavarna Tsonko
Tsonev and with a number of representatives of municipalities such as Varna and

Vratsa. Unfortunately, this idea was not realized due to Meredith's death.

William Meredith died on May 30, 2007 in New Landon.

After his death, his home in Uncasville on the banks of the River Thames was declared a cultural monument and seat of the newly established William Meredith Foundation with President R. Harteis . The Foundation has been active. Annually he hands a poetry award to William Meredith, and his books are included in the plans of the Foundation's Publishing House. This prestigious award was awarded to prominent artists Andrew Orkney, Gray Jakobik, Peter Maine, James Bale. The award "William Meredith" was received in 2013 by Lyubomir Levchev for his poem "The Horse with Green Wings".

The International Plainner, organized by my wife and me, dedicated to the 130th anniversary of the Bulgarian Liberation from Ottoman rule, was attended by our poet Richard Chartais and Meredith's sculptor and close friend Nancy Frankel. The cities of Sofia, Dolni Lozen, Plovdiv, Batak, Chirpan,

Richard Hartays during the 20-day Pleven dedicated to the 130th anniversary of the Bulgarian Liberation from Ottoman rule.

Stara Zagora, Gurkovo, Kazanlak, Shipka, Pleven, Etropole, Pravets, Cherven Bryag, Svishtov, Bansko. During the festival, recitals with poems of Meredith and Chartais were organized in my translation. In the closing exhibition at the Gallery of the National Art Gallery in Sofia was presented the work of N. Frenkel. One of the most significant works of Richard Hartness on a Bulgarian subject is his poem "Plenter" inspired by Batak's visit during his 2009 participation in Bulgarian, Russian, Israeli and American artists dedicated to the 130- the anniversary of the liberation of Bulgaria from Turkish slavery.Our relationship with Richard and Nancy continues to this day.

Richard and Nancy during one of their visits to Bulgaria

On September 20, 2013, we organized a presentation of Richard Hartness at the Bogoridi Gallery in Burgas.

Richard Hartness, poetess Rosa Boyanova and me.

Over the years, we have come to see them coming to Bulgaria. Some are also related to future joint
plans.

On the way from Bourgas to Sofia.

In 2016, in fulfillment of W.Meridith's pre-death wish, part of the poet of the American poet was brought to his second home in Bulgaria and scattered by R. Hartais around the Rila Monastery.

On September 16, 2018, the Bulgarian Embassy in Washington DC was held jointly with the William Meredith Foundation evening dedicated to the upcoming centenary of an American poet. The Ambassador Tihomir Stoychev spoke at the evening and read the greeting sent by me. Richard Harteis and the cultural attache Tatiana Karadjova read Meredith's poems in my translation. Also exhibited with books by Poets Choise Publishing House. Peter Menge, Elizabeth Ritchie, the widow of Andrew Orksey, Grace Cavalieri, WM Riveira, Laura Brillowsky and Barbara Goldberg took part in the reception.

Photo from the evening of 16 September 2018 at the Embassy of Bulgaria in Washington.

It was a film about W.Meredith's life and work.

A series of events dedicated to W. Meredith's 100th anniversary will be organized during the anniversary year.

Today, looking at William Meredith's creativity and activity from the height of his 100th anniversary, we can not disagree with the words of American poet and literary critic Edward Hursh: "Meredith looks generous to our world. It does not conceal the tragic, unpredictable and endless difficulties we encounter. His poetry resonates with responsibility for such old-fashioned concepts as honor, morality, optimism, dignity and human happiness.

A Tribute

By Richard Harteis

Ten years ago, on May 30th, William Meredith died. "Now he belongs to the ages," it was said of Lincoln and later Kennedy when he died, – Kennedy would have been a 100 years old this year, and William will have his centenary in 2019. William didn't die for his country, but he lived and died for poetry. Though he is not the global icon Kennedy became, William's life and art continue to reverberate in American culture, indeed, the world, like circles spiraling out toward the shore when a stone is dropped into the center of a lake. The Irish writer Jack Harte has said, "William was one of America's greatest poets, but also a wonderful human being." In Bulgaria he received the country's highest honors. He has left his mark in visits to many cities around the world from New Delhi, and Paris, to St. Petersburg, Sarajevo and Athens. But he is the quintessentially American poet, a "nutmegger" whose spirit flourished in his native New England, and whose work ascertained the universal through the particularity of the American tribe he loved so dearly.

William served as a naval aviator in WWII and the Korean Conflict.
"I'd respect you for that if for nothing else," Robert Frost told him once when William described the thirty--two night landings he made on an aircraft carrier during the war. Years later, William and Stewart Udall talked the old man into reading at Kennedy's inauguration in what became an iconic moment for poetry in the US. More than anything, Meredith wished to be useful in the culture, he was not an ivory tower poet. And when he served as US Poet Laureate, one of his highest priorities was to involve the African American community in programs at the Library of Congress and work with high school teachers to help bring this art form to their students.

His was an extraordinary life. Poet, pilot, arborist (his home in Connecticut counted twelve sorts of beeches, grafted trees, and a secret formal garden with hemlock and boxwood hedges, Dogwoods and Umbrella Pines.) Poetry, trees and students were the three legs of the pedestal on which his life rested. He was a beloved teacher at Connecticut College for nearly four decades, was never happier than when balling and moving trees with his partner at the nursery, or perusing perhaps 30 drafts of a given poem – he enjoyed revisions, knew that it was in the re-writing that the writing occurred. He was awarded the Pulitzer Prize, the National Book Award and the LA Times Book Award, all of which came after the challenges of a major stroke, and his work has received many additional American and international awards. He was Chancellor and Director of the Academy of American Poetry and received numerous honorary doctorates. In 1996, he was accorded Bulgarian citizenship by President Zhelu Zhelev for the bridge he created between our two countries.

Too often, when the great ones die, they simply fall off the planet, a lifetime of achievement and wisdom lost. But the foundation named for him tries to carry on his legacy in American culture through educational programs and the publication of an annual poetry prize in his name. On the centennial anniversary of his birth in 2019, it plans a series of important readings and poetry events throughout the year. It will establish a translation prize in honor of William's translator and friend, Valentin Krustev to join the Meredith Award in poetry, now in its sixth year. It also plans to publish a memorial calendar for 2019 featuring archival photos from the Mystic Seaport with William's poems superimposed on the images. The foundation recently established an auxiliary press to publish books of poetry and prose: POETS-CHOICE.COM. These projects to be funded by a campaign benefiting the foundation's work:

https://www.gofundme.com/WilliamMeredithCentennial

For many, William Meredith is a model of courage, civility, and creative artistry. It is our hope that friends and lovers of poetry will join in celebrating this remarkable man in the coming months. A short poem by Meredith perhaps summarizes his philosophy best:

A Major Work **Poems**

are hard to read   Pictures

are hard to see Music is

hard to hear

And people are hard to love.

But whether from brute need

Or diving energy.

At last, mind eye and ear

And the great sloth heart will move.

USEFUL LINKS TO MEREDITH'S LIFE AND WORK AND THAT OF THE FOUNDATION

Website: http://www.WilliamMeredithFoundation.org

Governor's Award for Lifetime Achievement: https://www.youtube.com/watch?v=qugmOD162sA

Bulgarian National TV account of travel to Rila Monastery in Bulgaria with Meredith's ashes https://www.youtube.com/watch?v=Ryy2K3WTs9Y

Meredith Foundation film describing the work of the foundation https://www.youtube.com/watch?v=3nBNMlihMSE Part one https://www.youtube.com/watch?list=PLzOOuHyViMMyQOIBYMr--nr58YS--nDvLvlXy&v=nqT--n_mgOOI1s Part 2 https://www.youtube.com/watch?v=81tV--n5dyc0A&list=PLzOOuHyViMMyQOIBYMr--nr58YS--n_DvLvlXy&index=2 Part 3 https://www.youtube.com/watch?v=i_thMVLbfWM&list=PLzOOuHyViMMyQOIBYMr--nr58YS--n_DvLvlXy&index=3

• Drunken Boat--nIn depth feature article on Meredith in a fine on--nline literary magazine: http://www.drunkenboat.com/db7/feature--nmeredith/index.html

• Connecticut College webpage with full accounting of his life, works, etc. http://collections.conncoll.edu/meredith/

William reading his poem, "Crossing Over" circa 1964: https://www.youtube.com/watch?v=IJM8SU--nrRP0

Meredith page from the Academy of American Poets: https://www.youtube.com/watch?v=IJM8SU- -nrRP0

The Poetry Foundation page on Meredith: https://www.poetryfoundation.org/poems-and-poets/poets/detail/william-meredith

Wikipedia page for Meredith: https://en.wikipedia.org/wiki/William_Morris_Meredith_Jr.

Auxiliary press established by the foundation for publications: Poets-choice.com

Love Song for William Meredith
By Julia Alvarez

When I landed at Connecticut College (then, "for women") in 1967, I was delighted to discover there was such a thing as creative writing. I don't think that term was being used back then. More likely, the title of the course would have been "Writing Poetry," a workshop taught by William Meredith (whom I also had never heard of). To be sure the William Meredith I got to know would have objected to his course being called "creative writing." He would have said that all good writing was of the creative kind.

I was a youngster in that classroom in a number of ways. First, I was a freshman (as we women were known back then), and a young one at that, seventeen when I started college. I was also an immigrant, only "seven American years old," as I dated my life in English, beginning in the summer of 1960 when we had fled the dictatorship of Trujillo and landed in New York City.

Because I wasn't confident in my new language, I reverted to reading the language of the body: facial expressions, posture, tone of voice, and so on. I watched my teachers closely, trying to understand their subtle reactions, where I stood on their measure of excellence, where I was falling short. Even here, I often ran into trouble as I was used to effusive and expressive Latin faces. Mr. Meredith's especially presented a challenge. He had a quiet, reserved manner, and an odd smile, a kind of twisting/listing of his mouth to one side that I misunderstood as a smirk of disdain or disapproval.

There was a modesty to his demeanor and dress: he wore a seersucker jacket (I recall learning what seersucker was when a student described his jacket), often with a tie. He spoke in such a soft voice, I felt myself leaning in to catch his every word. Sometimes, he seemed to be daydreaming, looking out the window, while some student read her poem. I had a sense that he didn't miss anything. His comments must have been witty (the smart kids in class snickered). I felt I was barely keeping up.

Since I couldn't read him, I decided to read his work. I went the library and took out two of his books, *The Open Sea* and *The Wreck of the Thresher*. I had never heard of *buying* poetry books--where would I even go to buy one and with what spending money?--my immigrant parents were still struggling. I read and reread Mr. Meredith's books. Back then, a carryover from childhood when we had to recite poems at school and for company, any poem I loved I committed to memory. (I loved the term in English "know by heart.") Of all Meredith's poems, my favorite was "The Open Sea." Its lines were the perfect subtitles for my growing confusion and anguish as to where I belonged and who was I going to be in my new country. I felt torn apart by competing allegiances: no longer fully Dominican, nor yet American, a lonely place. *We say the sea is lonely, better say/ourselves are lonesome creatures whom the sea/gives neither yes or no for company.* I recited the poem over and over for company. In class now whenever Mr. Meredith gazed out the window, a cartoon bubble blew up above his head. (*Oh, there are people, all right, settled in the sea--/It is as populous as Maine today/But no one who will give you the time of day.*)

Mr. Meredith introduced me to the work of a number of poets, not just dead ones. I recall Louise Bogan, Delmore Schwartz, John Berryman, Maxine Kumin, Howard Nemerov, Richard Wilbur, Muriel Rukeyser. We read a lot of Frost (*Two roads diverged in a yellow wood*) as well as T.S. Eliot whose "Love Song of J. Alfred Prufrock" was my absolute favorite (*I grow old. . . I grow old. . . I shall wear the bottoms of my trousers rolled. . . .* So, was the quiet, unassuming Mr. Meredith J. Alfred Prufrock? I remember wondering). The more I read, the greater my sense of my own ineptitude. English was not my mother tongue. I would never catch up.

And so, I was surprised when at the end of the semester, Mr. Meredith encouraged me to take a workshop with a young Black poet who would be replacing him during his upcoming sabbatical year, June Jordan. (Someone else I had never heard of.) He also recommended I look into the Bread Loaf Writers' Conference, a ten-day gathering of writers in Vermont, where he was on the staff. Wow! I had never heard of such a thing. A whole conference with other people who loved poetry as much as I did. Maybe I would find my true homeland there.

Of course, I followed Mr. Meredith's advice. I signed up for June Jordan's poetry workshop as well as her course on Revolution and Literature. (I recall another young writer, quiet, intense, supremely shy, Gayle Jones, and the pride we both felt as co-winners of the department's poetry prize.) I also applied to the Bread Loaf Writers' Conference, where, it turned out, many of the poets whose poems we had read in Mr. Meredith's class were also on the staff: Maxine Kumin, Robert Hayden, John Ciardi, Archibald MacLeish. Mr. Meredith had been right on both counts. June Jordan's workshop brought me down from the ivory tower of poetry (*I must lie down where all the ladders start/ in the foul rag and bone shop of the heart*). Her poems gave me courage (*These poems/they are things that I do/in the dark/reaching for you/whoever you are/... whoever I might become*) and she encouraged me to trust my own voice with its expressive Latin roots and rhythms (*I know it's been said before/but not in this voice/of the plátano/and the mango,/ marimba y bongó,/not in this sancocho/of inglés/con español*). At Bread Loaf, I found kindred spirits and fell in love with Robert Frost country. That same fall, right after my summer at the conference, I transferred to Middlebury College, so that when Mr. Meredith returned to Connecticut College from his sabbatical, I was already gone. turned to Connecticut College from his sabbatical, I was already gone.

Looking back, I think inviting June Jordan, as well as other poets of color and female writers to the still-staid all-women Connecticut College signaled Mr. Meredith's own broadening of subject matter and adoption of a less formal style. I recall my surprise and delight reading the new poems in *Earth Walk* (1970) and *Hazard, the Painter* (1975) and discovering his versatility and ability to enter a diversity of points of view. Keats' negative capability in action. In "Walter Jenks' Bath," the speaker is a Black boy in Beloit contemplating himself and the universe during his nightly bath—a far stretch from the poet professor I'd known in his seersucker jacket and tie (since replaced by love beads). Subsequent summers at Bread Loaf, he seemed looser, more radical—we were at the height of the Vietnam War—though always, Mr. Meredith's sense of fine balance and propriety, his irony and kindness kept him from the stridency of his more vehement colleagues.

Our lives briefly crossed again in an indirect way. The fall of my senior year at Middlebury, to my Dominican parents' dismay, I fell foolishly in love with a local boy--and he really was just a boy, seventeen years old, a high-school-dropout folk musician. After not having any luck enlisting my Middlebury College professors in her crusade, Mami contacted Mr. Meredith, remembering how much I revered my poetry teacher and quoted his advice--especially whenever I wanted my parents to let me do something they would not normally approve of, like go to a coed writers' conference.

In her letter to him, my mother explained that I was ruining my life with an uneducated, hippy, pot-smoking folk musician, and all my talent going to waste. (First I heard that my mother thought I had talent.) Would Mr. Meredith please try to talk some sense into me? Instead, William Meredith wrote my mother back, a letter she later showed me after we reconciled and she forgave me for ruining my life, code for having sex with my boyfriend. It was a short, typed missive on stiff white stationary, like a wedding invitation, in which Mr. Meredith kindly but firmly set my mother straight: whether I would stay with poetry or not, it was up to me and only me. We cannot someone else's star. To that effect. Needless to say, Mami was not happy with this response. (*A man who asks there of his family/ Or a friend or teacher gets a cold reply. . .)*

I didn't see Mr. Meredith again until years later in Washington, D.C. I had just won the Jenny McKean Moore Writing fellowship at George Washington and published my first book of poems, *Homecoming* (1984). As part of the fellowship, I had to give a "public reading," and guess who showed up? Mr. Meredith! What a shock! He was in a wheelchair. It was difficult to understand his garbled speech, but his partner, Richard Harteis, filled me in on the details. Mr. Meredith had had a stroke and was having trouble recalling words and speaking. Hearing of his affliction, which must be a poet's worst fear, I felt a stab of pity and dread. But Mr. Meredith was optimistic. He would lick this thing. ("I'm in bad health, but high spirits," he remarked to one interviewer.) He and Richard were in D.C. for some do or other at the Library of Congress, where he had recently been consultant in poetry, a position later retitled, Poet Laureate. They had heard I was giving a reading and decided to surprise me. Maybe because I now had more confidence in my work and in interacting with him, Mr. Meredith ("Call me, William") seemed more accessible than I'd ever remembered him. In fact, his affection and warmth were palpable, and though I had trouble understanding him, I had a ready supply of his own words to fill in the many blanks in his utterances. *(Poetry makes such things happen/ sometimes, as certain people do/ at the right juncture of our lives.))*

From then on, we never lost touch. Thanks to his former student and friend (and mine) and literary godchild, the poet Michael Collier, who became director of Bread Loaf in 1994, Mr. Meredith was a regular visitor when the conference was in session. I was now a writer-in-residence down the road at Middlebury College. Every time Michael alerted me, I made a point of driving up the mountain to see my dear old teacher. His speech had improved--at any rate, it was easier for me to understand him. We talked about writing, about the conference, about his travels—he spoke of trips to the former Yugoslavia, several to Bulgaria, southern France, all of which made me marvel at how he got around. We hugged in greeting and hugged and kissed in departure--something my seventeen-year- old self would not have believed possible. We exchanged letters. Usually, it was Richard who wrote back with the news; at the end, in his shaky handwriting, a note from Mr. Meredith. (I never did make that transition he urged on me to "William.) "Shame on you!" Richard chastised me in one letter. "You made an old man cry a little with your sweet note."

"I'm speaking well now, love, William," Mr. Meredith closed.

In 2007, fittingly a few days after Memorial Day, I learned that Mr. Meredith had died. It might have been Michael Collier who wrote me an email. I hope so. I would not have wanted to hear of our literary godfather's passing from anything as impersonal as a news report. On a shelf above my writing table, I still keep the photo of Mr. Meredith and myself that someone snapped at Bread Loaf in 1994, the two of us talking, making that supreme effort at speech, at getting the words right, what he spent a lifetime doing, in poems and in his life, and which I'm now closing in on a lifetime of doing myself.

I am grateful to Michael Collier for giving me this opportunity to recall our teacher and friend. The very day I began writing this piece, I received a note from Michael saying, "Today is William's 100th birthday." That night I had a dream in which Mr. Meredith and I were walking together on a path in the woods. (Gone was the wheelchair!) We came to a parting of ways. Knowing how, *"way leads on to way,"* I felt some urgency to tell him how much he meant to me. I stirred awake and jotted down the few words I recalled saying to him: *Mr. Meredith: I followed the path because you showed me the way, and that way led through words, and the words led to love.* Something to that effect. In the dream, I remember hoping my love song would detain him or elicit some reply. But true to form, Mr. Meredith was quiet, listening. He had already given me his reply in poems I still love and know by heart.

Julia Alvarez

Julia Alvarez, author of *How the García Girls Lost Their Accents* and *In the Time of the Butterflies*, celebrates the legacy of Pulitzer Prize–winning poet William Meredith, who taught at Conn from 1955 to 1983. In April, Conn celebrated the centennial of Meredith's birth.

PHOTO GALLERY

Join the William Meredith Foundation in celebrating its 2019 awardees in conjunction with *Nancy at Ninety: A Retrospective of Form and Color*, an exhibition of work by DC-based sculptor Nancy Frankel. Bulgarian Ambassador Tihomir Stoytchev will present two award-winning publications by the Meredith Foundation with readings by the awardees. Tom Kirlin will receive the 2019 Meredith Award for Poetry, and the Valentin Krustev Award for Translation to renowned DC poet and translator, Barbara Goldberg, for her translations of Israeli poetry. Refreshments will be served. Free and open to all, please RSVP to MarathonFilm@gmail.com.

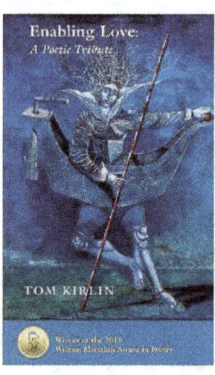

Image: Nancy Frankel, *Impromptu*, 2010. Steel, 33 x 33 x 11 in. Courtesy of the Artist.

4400 Massachusetts Ave NW,
Washington, DC

(202) 885-1300

www.american.edu/museum

The American Univeristy Museum Hours:
11AM–4PM, Tuesday–Sunday, Closed Mondays

Admission is free

Parking is available under the Katzen Arts Center
Free after 5PM and on weekends.

For more information on current and upcoming
exhibitions and events, please visit us online.

Valentin Krustev with William Meredith at Waterford Beach

Richard Harteis and William at Texas Falls, Bread Loaf

Visiting Lyubomir Levchev at his home in Sofia

Robert Frost and William at Princeton, 1940?

William Meredith, President Zhelu Zhelev, and Richard Harteis receive Bulgarian citizenship

Richard Harteis, William Meredith and blind soothsayer, Baba Vanga

Stoimen Stoilov, Connie Bozhilov, William Meredith in Varna in the late 1970's

Bread Loaf: Michael and Katherine Collier with William Meredith

Archangel Richard and Superman William with Daisy

Visiting in Connemara after a little accident

visiting American Ambassador Tom Foley on the first day of our visit to Ireland.

Drinks with Seamus ("the famous") Heaney in Dublin

Pensive William in the window of Yeats' tower

Dublin Streets

Art opening in New Haven with Curator Johnes Ruta

William on the wing of his plane in WWII

Bob Dole greets William at WWII memorial celebration

Bill Barrett and William at Emily Clayton Point at Riverrun
shortly after William's stroke.   Photo by Emma Rodrigues

Ellen Bettmann writes: "My whole life was shaped by William's having been my teacher at CC. It changed Michael's life too.

When we named our first child William that decision said a lot, but anointing WMM with the satin A at graduation was a treasured moment because it allowed me to make my gratitude and love a big fat public event

Nancy Frankel at the dedication of her sculpture

William at the Capitol Hill apartment during his time at the LIbrary of Congress as US Poet Laureate. Back of photo inscription to Bill Barrett who lived across the hall.

> In a characteristic pose, the guru's mouth is temporarily closed but he holds up the pale crystal lotus blossom.
>
> For Barrett with love
> William
> '75

Writers' Conference, Sandy Taylor in Sofia

Writers Union House in Varna, Bulgaria. Cheeky little Rusky

St Patrick's Day in West Palm Beach with Daisy

Actual shot of William in lead plane in WWII

Visiting Dave Halliday's farm near the Canadian Border during the funeral weekend celebration of his mother's life, Alice Halliday, expert biologist on the Manhattan project.

Three Santas in their red sleigh

Thresher Memorial dedication, New London Public Library

William at Coole Park Ireland

Harry and Catherine Hull

I will arise and go now, for always night and day

I hear lake water lapping with low sounds by the shore; While I

stand of the roadway, or on the pavement grey I hear it in the deep

heart's core.

        The lake Isle of Innisfree, July 2006

William signing his poem, "Notre Dame de Chartres" in his hotel with the cathedral in the window background.

Happy Birthday William, West Palm Beach

Ed Hirsch and Michael Collier at Bread Loaf

Betty Lussiner in Staten Island

Feeding the swans after a jog along Kitemaug Road

New Years Celebration with Jimmy Merrill at Riverrun

Kolyo Sevov in Varna, "Two Masks Unearthed in Bulgaria"

Lucinen Dimitrov, Nancy Frankel, Richard and Valentin Krustev in Blagoevgrad

Meeting with President Gerogi Parvanov in his office in Sofia

Red Square: in the footsteps of Robert Frost

Summer at Svetlana's Beach in Waterford

With Richard Wilbur inaugurating the Butterfly House in Key West

Ludmilla Zhivokova, Minister of Culture in Sofia who opened Bulgaria to the west. Lyubomir Levchev to William's left in this photo.

Visiting Yeats' tomb in Ireland with Jack Harte

India, 2000

Charles Chu

Don and Nathalie Black

Barbara and Dr. George Kraft

Elka Nyagolova, Maria Jouanic, RH, Nicky Prodanov, Nancy Frankel, Sara, Krassin Himmirski, Audrey Garbisch

William's father and Grandfather

Sandy and Peg Martin at Bread Loaf

Wretha Wiley Hanson

Letter from William to Richard, 1980

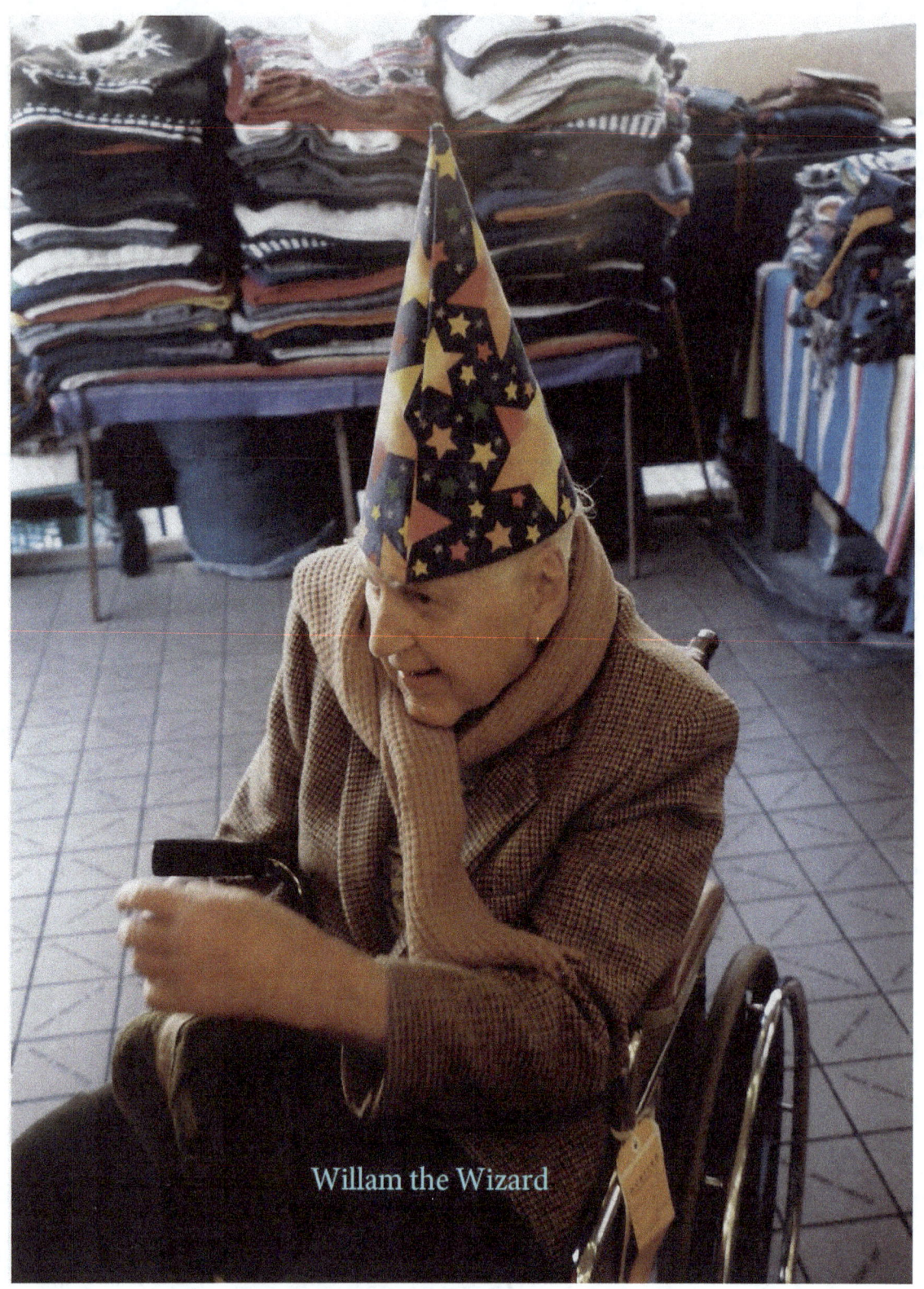
Willam the Wizard

www.ingramcontent.com/pod-product-compliance
Lightning Source LLC
Chambersburg PA
CBHW051403070526
44584CB00023B/3272